HAIRSTYLES
BRAIDING & HAIRCARE

HAIRSTYLES
BRAIDING & HAIRCARE

JACKI WADESON

Special Photography Alistair Hughes

HERMES HOUSE

This edition published by Hermes House

© Anness Publishing Limited 1999, 2004, 2005

Hermes House is an imprint of Anness Publishing Ltd
Hermes House, 88–89 Blackfriars Road, London SE1 8HA
tel. 020 7401 2077; fax 020 7633 9499; info@anness.com

Publisher: Joanna Lorenz
Project Editors: Casey Horton, Sarah Duffin, Joanne Rippin
Designer: Ruth Prentice, Bill Mason
Illustrator: Cherril Parris
Production Controller: Wanda Burrows
Hair Dressing Projects:
Photographer Alistair Hughes, assistant Neil Guegan
Hair: Kathleen Bray, assisted by Wendy MB Cook, Andrew Simmonds
Make-up: Vanessa Haines, Teresa Fairminer, Gigi
Models: Amanda, Christina, Carley, Laura Emily, Frieda, Hannah, Juliet, Zonna,
Fung-ling, Nicole, Carey, Bonnie, Anna, Maria, Sarah, Oihana, Krista, Ksnia,
Marcella, Anna, Tram, Silver, Penny, Sarah.

Clothes from a selection at Empire; Electrical styling products from BaByliss, Braun, Carmen,
Hair Tools, Philips, Remington, Rowenta, Vidal Sassoon; Equipment and accessories from
Celeste, Denman, Head Gardener, Kent, Jackel & Co, Laughtons, Johnny Loves Rosie;
Lady Jayne, Molton Brown; Products from Andrew Collinge Salon Solutions, Aveda,
Bain de Terre, The Body Shop, Citre, Clynol, Daniel Galvin, Dome, Goldwell, John Frieda,
Joico, KMS, Lamaur, Lazartique, L'Oréal, Matrix Essentials, Neal's Yard Remedies, Nicky Clarke,
Ore-an, Paul Mitchell, Phytologie, Poly, Redkin, Revlon, Schwarzkopf, Silvikrin, St Ives,
Trevor Sorbie, Wella, Vidal Sassoon, Zotos; Wigs and hairpieces Rene of Paris from Trendco,
Hairaisers, Trevor Sorbie.

1 3 5 7 9 10 8 6 4 2

CONTENTS

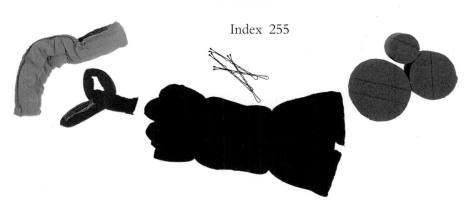

HEALTHY HAIR

BEAUTIFUL, SHINING HAIR IS A VALUABLE ASSET. IT CAN
ALSO BE A VERSATILE FASHION ACCESSORY, TO BE
COLOURED, CURLED, DRESSED UP, OR SMOOTHED
DOWN – ALL IN A MATTER OF MINUTES. HOWEVER, TOO
MUCH ATTENTION, COMBINED WITH THE EFFECTS OF A
POOR DIET, POLLUTION, AIR-CONDITIONING AND
CENTRAL HEATING, CAN MEAN THAT YOUR HAIR
BECOMES THE BANE OF YOUR LIFE RATHER THAN YOUR
CROWNING GLORY. A DAILY HAIRCARE ROUTINE AND
PROMPT TREATMENT WHEN PROBLEMS ARISE ARE
THEREFORE OF VITAL IMPORTANCE IN MAINTAINING THE
NATURAL BEAUTY OF HEALTHY HAIR.

THE STRUCTURE OF HAIR

A human hair consists mainly of a protein called keratin. It also contains some moisture and the trace metals and minerals found in the rest of the body. The visible part of the hair, called the shaft, is composed of dead tissue: the only living part of the hair is its root, the dermal papilla, which lies snugly below the surface of the scalp in a tube-like depression known as the follicle. The dermal papilla is made up of cells that are fed by the bloodstream.

Each hair consists of three layers. The outer layer, or cuticle, is the hair's protective shield and has tiny overlapping scales, rather like tiles on a roof. When the cuticle scales lie flat and neatly overlap, the hair feels silky-soft and looks glossy. If however, the cuticle scales have been physically or chemically damaged or broken, the hair will be dull and brittle and will tangle easily.

Under the cuticle lies the cortex, which is made up of fibre-like cells that give hair its strength and elasticity. The cortex also contains the pigment called melanin, which gives hair its natural colour. At the centre of each hair is the medulla, consisting of very soft keratin cells interspersed with spaces. The actual function of the medulla is not known, but some authorities believe that it carries nutrients and other substances to the cortex and cuticle. This could explain why hair is affected so rapidly by changes in health.

Hair's natural shine is supplied by its own conditioner, sebum, an oil composed of waxes and fats and also containing a natural antiseptic that helps fight infection. Sebum is produced by the sebaceous glands present in the dermis. The glands are linked to the hair follicles and release sebum into them. As a lubricant, sebum gives an excellent protective coating to the entire hair shaft, smoothing the cuticle scales and helping hair retain its natural moisture and elasticity. The smoother the surface of the cuticle, the more light will be reflected from the hair, and

HAIR STRUCTURE

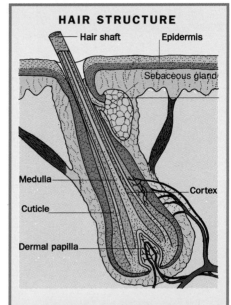

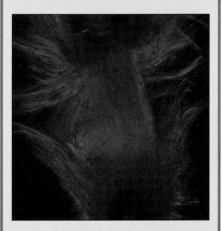

Centre and above: Pictures of a human hair magnified 200 times. A strand of hair in good condition is smooth, but if it has been damaged the outer layer is frayed and broken. Photographs courtesy of Redken Laboratories.

therefore, the higher will be the gloss. This is why it is more difficult to obtain a sheen on curly hair than on straight hair. Under certain circumstances, for example excessive hormonal activity, the sebaceous glands produce too much sebum, and the result is greasy hair. Conversely, if too little sebum is produced, the hair will be dry.

THE GROWTH CYCLE

The only living part of hair is underneath the scalp – when the hair has grown through the scalp it is dead tissue. Hair goes through three stages of growth: the anagen phase when it actively grows; the catagen, or transitional phase, when the hair stops growing but cellular activity continues in the papilla; and the telogen, or resting phase, when growth stops completely. During the telogen phase there is no further growth or activity at the papilla; eventually the old hair is pushed out by the new growth and the cycle begins again. The anagen phase continues for a period of two to four years, the catagen phase for only about 15–20 days, and the telogen phase for 90–120 days. At any given time, about 93 per cent of an individual's hair is in the anagen phase, 1 per cent is in the catagen phase, and 6 per cent is in the telogen phase. Scalp

FACT FILE
○ Hair grows about 1 cm/½ in per month.
○ A single strand lives for up to seven years.
○ If a person never had their hair cut it would grow to a length of about 107 cm/42 in before falling out.
○ Women have more hair than men.
○ Hair grows faster in the summer and during sleep.
○ Hairs grows fastest between the ages of 16 and 24 years.
○ Between the ages of 40 and 50 years women tend to lose about 20 per cent of their hair.
○ Hair becomes drier with age.

hair, which reacts to hormonal stimuli just like the hair on the rest of the body, is genetically programmed to repeat its growth cycle 24–25 times during the average person's lifetime.

THE IMPORTANCE OF DIET

What you eat is soon reflected in the health of your hair. Like the rest of the body, healthy, shining hair depends on a good diet to ensure it is supplied with all the necessary nutrients for sustained growth and health. Regular exercise is also important as it promotes good blood circulation, which in turn ensures that vital oxygen and nutrients are transported to the hair root via the blood. Poor eating habits and lack of exercise are soon reflected in the state of the hair; even a minor case of ill-health will usually make the hair look limp and lacklustre.

An adequate supply of protein in the diet is essential. Good sources include lean meat, poultry, fish, cheese and eggs as well as nuts, seeds and pulses. Fish, seaweed, almonds, Brazil nuts, yogurt and cottage cheese all help to give hair strength and a natural shine.

Wholegrain foods and those with natural oils are highly recommended for the formation of keratin, the major component of hair. Seeds are a rich source of vitamins and minerals as well as protein. Try to eat at least three pieces of fruit a day – it is packed with fibre, vitamins and minerals. Avoid saturated fat, which is found in red meat, fried foods and dairy products. Choose skimmed or semi-skimmed milk rather than the full-fat varieties, and low-fat cheese and yogurt instead of full-fat cheese and cream. Substitute vegetable oils such as sunflower, safflower and olive for animal fats. These foods all provide nutrients that are essential for luxuriant hair.

If you eat a balanced diet with plenty of fresh ingredients you shouldn't need to take any supplementary vitamins to promote healthy hair growth.

PROMOTING HEALTHY HAIR

○ Cut down on tea and coffee – they are powerful stimulants that act on the nervous, respiratory and cardiovascular systems, increasing the excretion of water and important nutrients. They also hamper the absorption of minerals crucial for hair health. Drink mineral water (between six and eight glasses a day), herbal teas and unsweetened fruit juice.

○ Alcohol dilates blood vessels and so helps increase blood flow to the tissues. However, it is antagonistic to several minerals and vitamins that are vital for healthy hair. Limit yourself to an occasional drink.

○ Regular exercise stimulates the circulatory system, encouraging a healthy blood supply to all cells and nourishing and helping to regenerate and repair.

○ Some contraceptive pills deplete B-complex vitamins and zinc. If you notice a change in your hair after starting to take the Pill, or changing brands, ask your **family doctor or nutritionist for advice.**

COLOUR

Hair colour is closely related to skin colour, which is governed by the same type of pigment, melanin. The number of melanin granules in the cortex of the hair and the shape of the granules determine a person's natural hair colour. In the majority of cases the melanin granules are elongated in shape. People who have a large number of elongated melanin granules in the cortex have black hair, those with slightly fewer elongated granules have brown hair, and people with even less will be blonde. In other people the melanin granules are spherical or oval in shape rather than elongated, and this makes the hair appear red.

Spherical or oval granules sometimes appear in combination with a moderate amount of the elongated ones, and then the person will have rich, reddish-brown tinges. If, however, spherical granules occur in combination with a large number of elongated granules, then the blackness of the hair will almost mask the redness, although it will still be present to give a subtle tinge to the hair and differentiate it from pure black.

Hair colour darkens with age, but at some stage in the middle years of life the pigment formation slows down and silvery-grey hairs begin to appear. Gradually, the production of melanin ceases, and all the hair becomes colourless – or what is generally termed grey.

When melanin granules are completely lacking from birth, as in albinos, the hair is pure white.

Hair colour is determined by the amount of pigment in the hair and the shape of the pigment granules. People with dark hair have a larger amount of pigment than people with blonde hair. In both brunettes and blondes the pigment granules are elongated: red hair results from the presence of oval-shaped granules. Photograph courtesy of Silvikrin.

Right: Red hair looks attractive whether it is worn smooth or curly. To create movement in longer hair, mist with styling lotion and set on shapers. If each strand of hair is twisted before winding, you will achieve a more fulsome curl.

Below left: Brunettes look good with precision bobs that are cut to increase volume in the hair. By Yosh Toya, San Francisco. Photography Gen.

Below right: This naturally curly blonde hair has been quickly styled by scrunch-drying to achieve maximum volume. By Nicky Clarke, London, Photography Paul Cox.

STRANGE BELIEFS

The Ancient Greeks regarded blonde as the hair colour of gods and heroes, but they viewed people with red hair with suspicion, and believed that strangers, rogues and redheads should be treated with contempt. The idea that redheads were untrustworthy, deceitful and quick-tempered was widespread in many cultures. In the Christian tradition Judas, who betrayed Christ, was said to have red hair, and artists of the early Christian period and beyond portrayed him as a redhead.

TEXTURE AND TYPE

Hair with a very curly texture needs intensive moisturizing treatments to keep the spring in the curl. On this type of hair always use a wide-toothed comb, never a brush, which will make the hair frizz. Leave-in conditioners are good for curly hair as they help to give curl separation. To revitalize curls, mist with water and scrunch with the hands.

ETHNIC DIFFERENCES

Scandinavians normally have thin, straight, baby-fine hair, and mid-Europeans have hair that is neither too fine nor too coarse. People native to the Indian subcontinent have coarse textured tresses, while Middle-Eastern populations have strong hair. In general, the further east you travel the coarser the hair becomes. The hair of Chinese and Japanese people is very straight; that of Latin-speaking and North African peoples can be very frizzy and thick.

The texture of your hair is determined by the size and shape of the hair follicle, which is a genetic trait controlled by hormones and related to age and racial characteristics.

Whether hair is curly, wavy or straight depends on two things: its shape as it grows out of the follicle and the distribution of keratin-producing cells at the roots. When viewed in cross-section, straight hair tends to be round; wavy hair tends to be oval; and curly hair kidney-shaped. Straight hair is formed by roots that produce the same number of keratin cells all round the follicle. In curly hair, however, the production of keratin cells is uneven, so that at any given time there are more cells on one side of the oval-shaped follicle than on the other. Furthermore, the production of excess cells alternates between the sides. This causes the developing hair to grow first in one direction and then in the other. The result is curly hair.

The natural colour of hair also affects the texture. Natural blondes have finer hair than brunettes, while redheads have the thickest hair.

Generally speaking, hair can be divided into three categories: fine, medium, and coarse and thick. Fine hair can be strong or weak; however, because of its texture, all fine hair has the same characteristic – it lacks volume. As the name suggests, medium hair is neither too thick nor too thin, and is strong and elastic. Thick and coarse hair is abundant and heavy, with a tendency to grow outwards from the scalp as well as downwards. It often lacks elasticity and is frizzy.

A single head of hair may consist of several different textures. For example, fine hair is often found on the temples, and the hairline at the front and on the nape of the head, while the texture over the rest of the head may be medium or even coarse.

NORMAL, DRY OR OILY?

Hair type is determined by the hair's natural condition – that is, by the amount of sebum the body produces. Treatment programmes such as perming, colouring and heat styling will also have an effect on hair type. Natural hair types and those produced by applying various treatments are described below, together with advice on haircare where appropriate.

Normal hair is neither greasy nor dry, has not been permed or coloured, holds its style, and looks good most of the

Thick, straight hair can be made sleeker if you remember to always blow-dry downwards, which encourages the cuticles to lie flat and reflect the light. Photograph courtesy of Braun.

Fine hair needs expert cutting to maximize the volume. Here, gel spray was used to give lift at the roots and the hair was then blow-dried. By Taylor Ferguson, Scotland.

Normal hair responds well to regular brushing, smoothing and polishing. By Antoinette Beenders at Trevor Sorbie, London, for Denman. Photography by Simon Bottomley.

time. Normal hair is ideally suited to the daily use of two-in-one conditioning shampoos. These are formulated to provide a two-stage process in one application. When the product is lathered into wet hair the shampoo removes dirt, grease and styling products. At this stage the conditioner remains in the lather. As the hair is rinsed with more water, the grease and dirt are washed away. At the the same time, the micro-fine conditioning droplets are released on to the hair, leaving it shiny and easy to comb.

Dry hair looks dull, feels dry, tangles easily, and is difficult to comb or brush, particularly when it is wet. It is often quite thick at the roots but thinner, and sometimes split, at the ends.
Causes Excessive shampooing, overuse of heat-styling equipment, misuse of colour or perms, damage from the sun, or harsh weather conditions. Each of these factors depletes the moisture content of hair, so that is loses its elasticity, bounce and suppleness. Dryness can also be the result of a sebum deficiency on the

hair's surface, caused by a decrease in, or absence of, sebaceous gland secretions.
Solutions Use a nourishing shampoo and an intensive conditioner (see Getting into Condition). Allow hair to dry naturally whenever possible.

Greasy hair looks lank and oily and needs frequent washing.
Causes Overproduction of sebum as a result of hormone disturbances, stress, hot, humid atmosphere, excessive brushing, or constantly running hands through the hair, perspiration, or a diet rich in saturated fat. The hair becomes oily, sticky and unmanageable in just a few days, or sometimes within hours.
Solutions Use a gentle, non-aggressive shampoo that also gives the hair volume. A light perm will lift the hair at the roots and limit the dispersal of sebum. Rethink your diet: reduce dairy fats and greasy foods. Try to eat plenty of fresh food, and drink six to eight glasses of water every day.

Combination hair is greasy at the roots but dry and sometimes split at the ends.

Causes Chemical treatments, using detergent-based shampoos too frequently, overexposure to sunlight, and overuse of heat-styling equipment. Such repeated abuse often provokes a reaction in sebum secretion at the roots and a partial alteration in the scales, which can no longer fulfil their protective role. The hair ends therefore become dry.
Solutions Use products that have only a gentle action on the hair. Excessive use of formulations for oily hair and those for dry hair may contribute to the problem. Ideally use a product specially designed for combination hair. If this is not possible try using a shampoo for oily hair and finish by applying a conditioner only from the middle lengths to the ends of the hair.

Coloured or permed hair is very often more porous than untreated hair, so it needs gentle cleansers and good conditioners. Colour-care products help prevent fading by protecting the hair from damaging rays of sunlight. Specialist products for permed hair help maintain elasticity, by giving longer lasting results.

THE CUT

Before, our model's fine hair tended to look flat and lank. Trevor Sorbie explained that by lightly layering, it could be made to look fuller and thicker.

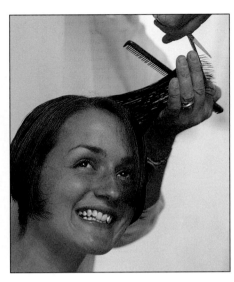

Hair is shampooed and conditioned and the front section cut, holding out at an angle from the head.

Trevor works his way through the crown area, cutting in a similar way which will make the hair easier to style.

Hair growth varies over different parts of the head. This is why your cut can appear to be out of shape very quickly. As a general rule, a short, precision cut needs trimming every four weeks, a longer style every six to eight weeks. Even if you want to grow your hair long it is essential to have it trimmed regularly – at least every three months – to prevent splitting and keep the ends even.

Hairdressers use a variety of techniques and tools to make hair appear thicker, fuller, straighter, or curlier, whatever the desired effect. The techniques and tools they use are explained below.

Blunt cutting, in which the ends are cut straight across, is often used for hair of one length. The weight and fullness of the hair is distributed around the perimeter of the shape.

Clippers are used for close-cut styles and sometimes to finish a cut. Shaved clipper cuts are popular with teenagers.

This heavily layered, graduated bob was cut close into the nape, and then the shape of the hair was emphasized by using a vegetable colour to give tone and shine. By Trevor Sorbie, London.

Nape hair is trimmed from one ear right round to the other ear. To style, mousse is applied from roots to ends and the hair blow-dried straight using a vent brush.

To finish, Trevor combs through gel which banishes any frizziness. By Trevor Sorbie, London. Photography Alistair Hughes – courtesy of Best Magazine

Graduated hair is cut at an angle to give fullness on top and blend the top hair into shorter lengths at the nape.

Layering the hair evenly distributes the weight and fullness, giving a round appearance to the style.

Slide cutting (also called slithering or feathering) thins the hair. Scissors are used in a sliding action, backwards and forwards along the hair length. This technique is often done when the hair is dry.

Razor cutting creates softness, tapering, and internal movement so that the hair moves freely. It can also be used to shorten hair.

Thinning, either with thinning scissors or a razor, removes bulk and weight without affecting the overall length of the hair.

CLEVER CUTS

Fine, thin, flyaway hair can be given volume, bounce and movement by blunt cutting. Mid-length hair can benefit from being lightly layered to give extra volume, while short, thin hair can be blunt cut and the edges graduated to give movement.

Some hairdressers razor cut fine hair to give a thicker and more voluminous effect. It is best not to let fine hair grow too long. As soon as it reaches the shoulders it tends to look wispy.

Thick and coarse hair can be controlled by reducing the weight to give more style and direction. Avoid very short styles because the hair will tend to stick out. Try a layered cut with movement.

Layering also helps achieve height and eliminates weight. On shorter styles, the weight can be reduced with thinning scissors expertly used on the ends only.

Sometimes hair grows in different directions, which may cause styling problems. For example, a cow-lick is normally found on the front hairline and occurs when the hair grows in a swirl, backwards and then forwards. Clever cutting can redistribute the weight and go some way to solving this problem. A double crown occurs when there are two pivots of natural hair at the top of the head, rather than the usual one. Styles with height at the crown are most suitable here.

To maximize the effect of a widow's peak the hair should be taken in the reverse direction to the growth. This gives the impression of a natural wave.

For this style, the model's straight hair was cut so that it would swing back into shape with every movement of the head. The shine was improved by using a longer-lasting semi-permanent colour. By L'Oréal.

CUTTING CURLS

Curly hair can be tamed by an expert cut that follows the natural movement of the hair and helps wave formation.

Before

The model's hair was an outgrown, naturally curly, short cut. She wanted to define the shape and work with the natural curl as opposed to against it. Before cutting, the hair was shampooed and coloured using a deep-brown semi-permanent colour.

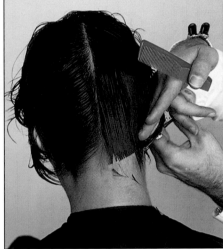

1 The hair was divided in half from crown to nape and cut from the natural point at the nape to behind the ear to create a strong line.

2 This process was repeated on the other side.

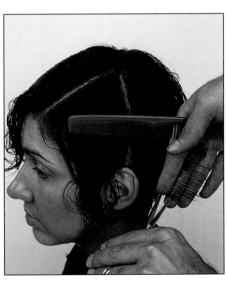

4 A box section was taken and left out on top of the head.

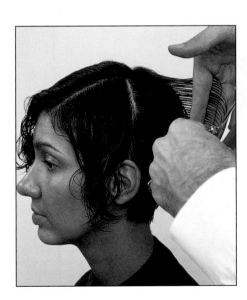

3 A section was taken from the crown to the occipital bone and cut to the desired length.

5 The hair was sectioned from the box section to the ear and cut to create softness around the ears.

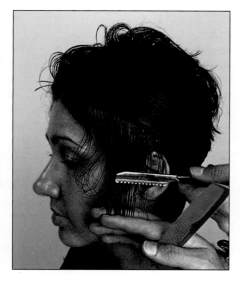

6 The box section was cut by point-cutting the corner off to create movement.

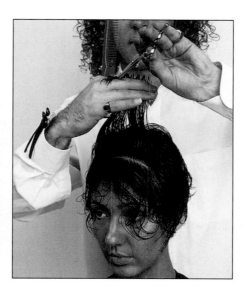

7 The top hair was cut.

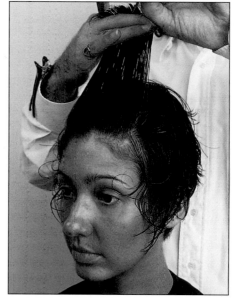

8 The fringe hair (bangs) was blended into the top.

9 The sides were blended into the back. Texturizing gel was worked through the hair which was then diffuser-dried. Photography Chris Bishop.

SHAMPOOING

S hampoos are designed to cleanse the hair and scalp, removing dirt and grime without stripping away too much of the natural sebum. They contain cleansing agents, perfume, preservatives and conditioning agents that can coat the hair shaft to make the hair appear thicker. The conditioning agents smooth the cuticle scales so the hair doesn't tangle, and help eliminate static electricity from the hair when it dries.

THE pH FACTOR

The letters pH refer to the acid/alkaline level of a substance. It is calculated on a scale of 1 to 14. Numbers below 7 denote acidity, those over 7, alkalinity. Most shampoos range between a pH factor of 5 and 7; medicated varieties have a pH of about 7.3, which is near neutral.

Sebum has a pH factor of between 4.5 and 5.5, which is mildly acidic. Bacteria cannot survive in this pH, so it is important to maintain this protective layer in order to keep the skin, scalp and hair in optimum condition.

Many shampoos are labelled "pH balanced", and this means they have the

Shampoos are available in different formulas to suit all hair types and conditions. Make sure you choose one that is right for your hair and use it as often as necessary to keep your hair clean. Rinse out the shampoo thoroughly. Photograph courtesy of Silvikrin.

SHAMPOO TIPS

❍ Use the correct shampoo (and not too much) for your hair type. If in doubt use the mildest shampoo you can buy.

❍ Don't wash your hair in washing-up liquid, soap or other detergents; they are highly alkaline and will upset your hair's natural pH balance by stripping out the natural oils.

❍ Read the instructions first. Some shampoos need to be left on the scalp for a few minutes before rinsing.

❍ If you can, buy small sachets of shampoo to test which brand is the most suitable for your hair.

❍ Never wash your hair in the bath; dirty bath water is not conducive to clean hair, and it is difficult to rinse properly without a shower attachment or separate jug.

❍ Always wash your brush and comb when you shampoo your hair.

❍ Change your shampoo every now and then; hair seems to develop a resistance to certain ingredients after a period of time.

❍ Don't throw away a shampoo that doesn't lather. The amount of suds is determined by the active level of detergent. Some shampoos have less suds than others but this has no effect on their cleansing ability. In fact, quite often, the more effective the product, the fewer the bubbles.

same acidity level as hair. Individuals with fragile, permed or coloured hair should use a shampoo of this type. However, for strong hair in good condition, a pH balanced shampoo is unnecessary, provided shampooing is followed by conditioning.

SHAMPOO SUCCESS

Always use a product formulated for your hair type - dry, normal, greasy or chemically treated - and before shampooing brush your hair to free any tangles and loosen dirt and dead skin cells. Use lukewarm water, as hot water can be uncomfortable.

Wet the hair, then apply a small amount of shampoo and gently massage into the roots, using the pads of your fingertips; never use your nails. Pay special attention to the hairline area, places where make-up and dirt become trapped. Allow the lather to work its way to the ends of the hair. Don't rub vigorously or you will stretch the hair.

When you have finished shampooing, rinse thoroughly until the water runs clean and clear. Repeat the process only if you think your hair needs it, again using only a small amount of shampoo. Finally, blot the hair with a towel to remove excess water before applying conditioner.

MASSAGING THE SCALP

Massage helps maintain a healthy scalp. It brings extra blood to the tissues, which enhances the delivery of nutrients and oxygen to the hair follicle. It also reduces scalp tension - which can contribute to hair loss - loosens dead skin cells, and helps redress the overproduction of sebum, which makes hair greasy.

You can give yourself a scalp massage at home. Use warm olive oil if the scalp is dry or tight. Try equal parts of witch hazel and mineral water if you have an oily scalp. For a normal scalp, use equal parts rose and mineral waters.

Begin the massage by gently rotating your scalp using the tips of

A head massage reduces scalp tension as well as promoting healthy hair growth. It is also a relaxing and pampering treatment that you can do yourself at home.

your fingers. Start at the forehead, move to the sides, and work over the crown to the nape of the neck. Then place your fingertips firmly on the scalp without exerting too much pressure. Push the fingers together then pull them apart through the hair in a kneading motion, without lifting or moving them. When you have massaged for about a minute, move to the next section. Continue until your entire scalp and upper neck have been treated.

ELABORATE HAIR STYLES

In the 17th and 18th centuries, hair washing was a biennial event. Fashionable women contrived towering heads of hair adorned with vegetables, fruit, feathers and even vases of flowers. Many ladies sat up all night dozing in chairs rather than spoil their headpieces by lying in bed.

GETTING INTO CONDITION

Long hair needs a regular conditioning regime to keep it healthy and shiny.
By Daniel Galvin, London, for L'Oréal Coiffure. Photography Iain Philpott.

In an ideal world, a regular shampoo would be sufficient to guarantee a glossy head of hair. Unfortunately, very few people are able to wash their hair and let the matter rest at that; most need some sort of help just to overcome the effects of modern living, not to mention the occasional problem that needs treatment. Here is a guide to the vast array of products available to get the hair in excellent condition.

THE CONDITIONERS

Glossy hair has cuticle scales that lie flat and neatly overlap, thus reflecting the light. Perming and colouring, rough handling and heat styling all conspire to lift the cuticles, allowing moisture to be lost from the cortex and making hair dry, lacklustre, and prone to tangle. Severely damaged cuticles break off completely, which means that the hair gets thinner and eventually breaks.

To put the shine back into hair and restore its natural lustre it may be necessary to use a specific conditioner that meets the hair's requirements. Conditioners, with the exception of hot oils, should be applied to freshly shampooed hair that has been blotted dry with a towel to remove excess moisture.

Today, there is a large, and sometimes confusing, number of conditioners on the market. The following list describes those which are widely available.

Basic conditioners coat the hair with a fine film, temporarily smoothing down the cuticle and making hair glossier and easier to manage. Leave for a few minutes before rinsing thoroughly.

Conditioning sprays are used prior to styling and form a protective barrier against the harmful effects of heat. They are also good for reducing static electricity on flyaway hair.

Hot oils give an intensive, deep nourishing treatment. To use, place the unopened tube in a cup of hot, tap water and leave to heat for one minute. Next, wet the hair and towel it dry before twisting off the tube top. Massage the hot oil evenly into the scalp and throughout the hair for one to three minutes. For a more intensive treatment, cover the head with a shower cap. To finish, rinse the hair, and shampoo.

Intensive conditioners help hair to retain its natural moisture balance, replenishing it where necessary. Use this type if the hair is split, dry, frizzy, or difficult to manage. Distribute the conditioner evenly through the hair and then allow it to penetrate for two to five minutes, or longer if required. Rinse very thoroughly with lots of fresh water, lifting your hair from the scalp to ensure any residue is washed away.

Leave-in conditioners are designed to help retain moisture, reduce static, and add shine. They are especially good for fine hair as they avoid conditioner overload, which can cause lankness. Convenient and easy to use, they also provide a protective barrier against the effects of heat styling. Apply after shampooing but don't rinse off. These products are ideal for daily use.

Restructurants penetrate the cortex, helping to repair and strengthen the inner part of damaged hair. They are helpful if the hair is lank and limp and has lost its natural elasticity as a result of chemical treatments or physical damage.

Split end treatments/serums condition damaged hair. The best course of action for split ends is to have the ends trimmed, but this does not always solve the whole problem because the hair tends to break off and split at different levels. As an intermediate solution, split ends can be temporarily sealed using these specialist conditioners. They should be worked into the ends of newly washed hair so that they surround the hair with a microscopic film that leaves the hair shaft smoother.

Colour/perm conditioners are designed for chemically treated hair. After-colour products add a protective film around porous areas of the hair, preventing colour loss. After-perm products help stabilize the hair, thus keeping the bounce in the curl.

PROBLEMS AND SOLUTIONS

Split ends, dandruff and dry, itchy scalp are common problems that can detract from otherwise healthy hair. In most cases such problems can be overcome by giving the appropriate treatment.

Dandruff consists of scaly particles with an oily sheen that lie close to the hair root. This condition should not be confused with a flaky scalp (see below).
Causes Poor diet, sluggish metabolism, stress, a hormonal imbalance and sometimes infection. These conditions produce increased cell renewal on the scalp, which is often associated with an increase in sebum. The scales will absorb the excess oil, but if the problem is untreated it will become worse.
Solutions Rethink your diet and lifestyle. Learn relaxation techniques if the problem appears to be caused by stress. Brush the hair before shampooing and scrupulously wash combs and brushes. Always choose a mild shampoo with an antidandruff action that gently loosens scales and helps prevent new ones. Follow with a treatment lotion, massaged into the scalp using the fingertips. The treatment must be used regularly if it is to be effective. Avoid excessive use of heat stylers. If the dandruff persists, consult your family doctor or trichologist.

Flaky/itchy scalp produces tiny, white pieces of dead skin that flake off the scalp and are usually first noticed on the shoulders. This condition can often be confused with dandruff but the two are not related. Sometimes the scalp is red or itchy and feels tense. The hair has a dull appearance.
Causes Hereditary traits, stress, insufficient rinsing of shampoo, lack of sebum, using a harsh shampoo, vitamin imbalance, pollution, air-conditioning and central heating.
Solutions Choose a moisturizing shampoo and a conditioner with herbal extracts to help soothe and remoisturize the scalp.

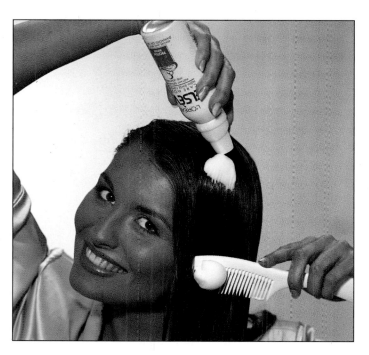

Leave-in conditioners that come in mousse formulations can be applied straight on to the hair from the container.

Use a styling comb with widely spaced teeth to distribute the conditioner from the roots to the ends of the hair. Do not rinse out, simply style and dry the hair as desired.

Above and right: Limp, fine hair can be transformed easily using a volumizing spray or thickening mousse before setting on large rollers. Make sure the hair is completely dry before removing rollers and lightly brushing the hair through. Hold with hairspray. By Nicky Clarke, London. Photography Paul Cox.

Fine hair tends to be limp, looks flat, and is difficult to style because it does not hold a style.

Causes The texture of fine hair is hereditary, but the problem is often made worse by using too heavy a conditioner, which weighs the hair down. Excessive use of styling products can have the same effect.

Solutions Wash hair frequently with a mild cleanser and use a very light conditioner. Volumizing shampoos can help give body, and soft perms will make hair appear thicker.

Frizzy hair results from the merest hint of rain or other air moisture being absorbed into the hair. It looks dry, lacks lustre, and is difficult to control.

Causes Can be inherited or caused by rough treatment, such as too much harsh brushing or pulling the hair into rubber bands.

Solutions When washing the hair, massage the shampoo into the roots and allow the lather to work its way to the ends. Apply a conditioner from the mid-lengths of the hair to the ends, or use a leave-in conditioner. The hair is often best styled with a gel, which should be applied when the hair is wet. Alternatively, allow the hair to dry naturally and then style it using a wax or pomade. Serums can also help. These are silicon-based products that work by surrounding the cuticle with a transparent microscopic film, which leaves the hair shaft smoother. Serums effectively prevent moisture loss and inhibit the absorption of dampness from the surrounding air.

Split ends occur when the cuticle is damaged and the fibres of the cortex unravel. The hair is dry, brittle and prone to tangling, and can split at the end or anywhere along the shaft.

Causes Over-perming or colouring, insufficient conditioning, or too much brushing or backcombing, especially with poor-quality combs or brushes. Careless use of spiky rollers and hair pins, excessive heat styling and not having the hair trimmed regularly, can also cause the problem.

Solutions Split ends can't be mended; the only long-term cure is to have them

snipped off. What is lost in the length will be gained in quality. It may help if you reduce the frequency with which you shampoo, as this in itself is stressful to hair and causes split ends to extend up the hair shaft. Never use a dryer too near the hair, or set it on too high a temperature. Minimize the use of heated appliances. Try conditioners and serums that are designed to seal split ends temporarily and give resistance to further splitting.

Product build-up is the residue of styling products and two-in-one shampoo formulation left on the hair shaft.

Causes When these residues combine with mineral deposits in the water, a build-up occurs preventing thorough cleansing and conditioning. The result is hair that is dull and lacks lustre; it is often difficult to perm or colour successfully because there is a barrier preventing the chemicals from penetrating the hair shaft. The colour can be patchy and the perm result uneven.

Solutions Use one of the stripping, chelating or clarifying shampoos, which are specially designed to remove product build-up. This is particularly important prior to perming or colouring.

Top left and above: Frizzy hair can be controlled using a moisturizing shampoo and conditioner. Style using a mousse designed for curly hair, which will help to eliminate tangles and reduce static. Finish with a few drops of serum to add a final touch of gloss. By Nicky Clarke, London. Photography Paul Cox.

Above left: Split ends can't be mended, just temporarily sealed. The only permanent cure is to have your hair trimmed regularly.

Natural ingredients such as herbs and essential oils can help you achieve beautifully conditioned hair. Here, a hot oil treatment was applied to the model's hair to enhance its shine and condition. Natural oils that are suitable for applying to the hair and scalp include vegetable oils, but rosemary, ylang-ylang and lavender essential oils are fragrant alternatives. Use according to the manufacturer's directions. By Daniel Galvin, London.

NATURAL SOLUTIONS

Since time immemorial, herbs and plants have been used to heal, pamper and beautify. Many of these age-old haircare recipes still apply today. The following are a few you might like to try at home. Remember to use them immediately after you have made them: they won't keep.

Dandruff solution

Mix a few drops of oil of rosemary with 30 ml/2 tbsp of olive oil and rub well into the scalp at bedtime. Shampoo and rinse thoroughly in the morning.

Egg shampoo

In a blender, mix together two small eggs with 50 g/2 oz of still, mineral water and 15 ml/1 tbsp of cider vinegar or lemon juice. Blend for 30 seconds at low speed. Massage well into the scalp and rinse very thoroughly using lukewarm water (if the water is any hotter the egg will begin to set).

Herbal shampoo

Crush a few dried bay leaves with a rolling pin and mix with a handful of dried camomile flowers and one of rosemary. Place in a large jug and pour over 1 litre/1¾ pints of boiling water. Strain after 2–3 minutes and mix in 5 ml/1 tsp of soft or liquid soap. Apply to the hair, massaging well. Rinse thoroughly.

Hot oil

Any vegetable oil is suitable for conditioning. Just heat the oil until slightly warm. Rub a little into your scalp and then through every part of your hair, massaging gently as you go. Cover your head with a plastic shower cap for 20 minutes; the heat from your head will help the oil penetrate the hair shaft. Shampoo and rinse thoroughly.

Intensive conditioning treatment

Warm 15 ml/1 tbsp each of wheat germ and olive oil and massage into the scalp. Wrap a warm towel around the head and leave for 10 minutes. Then rinse with a basin of water to which the juice of a lemon has been added.

Hair tonic

Beat 150 ml/5 fl oz of natural yogurt with an egg; add 5 ml/1 tsp of sea kelp powder and 5 ml/1 tsp of finely grated lemon rind. Mix thoroughly and work into the hair. Cover your hair with a plastic shower cap and leave in place for 40 minutes. Shampoo and rinse.

Using essential oils

Pure aromatherapy oils can be used for hair care. The following recipes come from world-famous aromatherapist, Robert Tisserand. The number of drops of oil, as listed, should be diluted in 30 ml/2 tbsp of vegetable oil, which will act as a carrier oil.

Dry hair: rosewood 9, sandalwood 6.
Oily hair: bergamot 9, lavender 6.
Dandruff: eucalyptus 9, rosemary 6.
Mix the required treatment and apply to dry or wet hair. Massage the scalp using the fingertips. Leave for two to five minutes. Shampoo and rinse thoroughly.

You can grow your own herbs or find them and other ingredients such as essential oils and henna, in many health-food shops and pharmacies. They are also available through specialist shops selling natural remedies and beauty products. Many hair treatments can be made safely, economically and easily at home.

HAIR RINSES

Lemon juice added to the rinsing water, will brighten blonde hair, while 30 ml/2 tbsp of cider vinegar will add gloss and body to any colour hair.

Other rinses (to be used after shampooing) can be made up to treat a variety of hair problems. First you must make an infusion by placing 30 ml/2 tbsp of a fresh herb in a china or glass bowl. Fresh herbs are best, but if you are using dried herbs remember they are stronger so you will need to halve the amount required for fresh herbs. Add 600 ml/1 pint boiling water, cover and leave to steep for three hours. The longer the herbs steep the stronger the infusion. Strain before using. Make infusions with the following herbs for the specific uses as listed:

○ Southernwood to combat grease.
○ Nettle to stimulate hair growth.
○ Rosemary to prevent static.
○ Lavender to soothe a tight scalp.

Make a parsley hair tonic (see picture right) by blending a large handful of parsley sprigs and 30 ml/2 tbsp water in a food processor until well puréed. Apply to the scalp, cover with a shower cap, and leave for an hour before rinsing thoroughly.

TIMES OF CHANGE

Hair goes through many different stages during a lifetime. Each stage brings with it different requirements in haircare. The most significant stages are described below, together with recommendations for promoting hair health during each phase.

BEGINNINGS:
THE BABY AND CHILD

A baby's hair characteristics are determined from the very moment of conception. By the 16th week of pregnancy the foetus will be covered with lanugo, a downy body hair that is usually shed before birth. The first hair appears on the head at around 20 weeks gestation and it is at this time that the pigment, melanin, which will determine the colour of the hair, is first produced.

A few weeks after birth, the baby's original hair begins to fall out or is rubbed off. The new hair is quite different from the initial downy mass, so a baby born with blonde, wispy curls might have dark straight hair by the age of six months.

Cradle cap, which appears as thick, yellow scales in patches over the scalp, causes many mothers concern. Cradle cap is the result of a natural build-up of skin cells. It is nothing to worry about and can be gently loosened by rubbing a little baby oil on to the scalp at night and washing it off in the morning. This may need to be repeated for several days until all the loose scales have been lifted and washed away.

Mothers often carefully trim their baby's hair as and when necessary, and it is not until the child is about two years of age that a visit to a hairdressing salon may be necessary. Children's hair is normally in beautiful condition and is best cut and styled simply.

At the onset of puberty, young adults suddenly become much more interested in experimenting with their hair. This is when they may experience greasy hair and skin for the first time. A re-evaluation of the shampoos and conditioners currently in use is often necessary to keep hair looking good.

HAIRCARE DURING
PREGNANCY

During pregnancy, the hair often looks its best. However after the birth, or after breast-feeding ceases, about 50 per cent of mothers experience what appears to be excessive hair loss. This is related to the three stages of hair growth (see page 8). During pregnancy and breast-feeding, hormones keep the hair at the growing stage for longer than usual, so it appears thicker and fuller. Some time after the birth – usually about 12 weeks later – this hair enters the resting stage, at the end of which all the hair that has been in the resting phase is shed. What appears to have been excessive hair loss is therefore simply a postponement of a natural occurrence, a condition that is known as post-partum alopecia.

A more significant problem that may occur during pregnancy is caused by a depletion in the protein content of the hair. As a result the hair becomes drier and more brittle. Combat this by frequent use of an intensive conditioning treatment.

GROWING UP

A baby's hair is soft and downy at first but it takes on its individual characteristics within six months of birth.

The toddler's hair requires a simple cut. At this stage the child is usually taken for his/her first visit to a salon.

Young boys need a hair cut that is easily combed into shape. By Regis, Europe.

Bobs suit most girls and are perfect for straight hair, but need regular trims. By Regis, Europe.

As women grow older the hair becomes thinner. A mid-length to short cut makes the hair less prone to droop. By Joseph and Jane Harling, Avon, England.

HAIR LOSS AND HRT

Medical opinion differs concerning the effect of Hormone Replacement Therapy (HRT) on the hair but it is generally accepted that in most cases it can be beneficial. However, trichologists advise that if women have had permanent hair thinning prior to taking HRT, the problem may be compounded. It is best to discuss this with your family doctor.

Avoid perming during pregnancy because the hair is in an altered state and the result can be unpredictable. However, a new colour can give your hair and your spirits a lift.

GROWING OLDER

With ageing, the whole body slows down, including the hair follicles, which become less efficient and produce hairs that are finer in diameter and shorter in length. Such shrinkage is gradual and the hair begins to feel slightly thinner, with less volume and density. At the same time, the sebaceous glands start to produce less sebum and the hair begins to lose its colour as the production of melanin decreases.

Blonde hair fades, brunettes lose their natural highlights, and redheads tone down to brownish shades. When melanin production stops altogether, the new hair that grows is white, not grey as is commonly perceived. The production of melanin is governed by genetic factors, and the best indication of when an individual's hair will become white is the age at which their parents' hair lost its colour. Pigment, apart from giving hair its colour, also helps to soften and make each strand more flexible. This is why white hair tends to become wirier and coarser in texture.

Because the texture changes, the hair is inclined to pick up dust and smoke from the atmosphere, so it soon appears to be discoloured and dirty.

This is particularly true for those who live in a town or spend time in smoky atmospheres. Cigarette smoke and natural gas from cookers discolour white hair and make it look yellow. Mineral deposits from chlorinated water can give white hair a greenish tinge. Chelating, clarifying, or purifying shampoos will help to strip this build-up from the hair.

To counteract dryness associated with ageing, use richer shampoos and conditioning products. As well as regular conditioning, weekly intensive treatments are essential to counteract moisture loss.

AS THE YEARS GO BY

Medium-textured hair that needs a lift can be given height on the crown with a root perm. By Paul Falltrick, Essex, England, for Clynol.

The hair has been cut to create more movement and softness. It was then scrunch-dried and finished with wax. By Regis, Europe.

Long hair was softened by feathering the sides and cutting a full fringe (bangs). A colour added gloss. By Nicky Clarke, London.

Fine, grey hair was highlighted and then toned using a rinse before blow-drying with a round brush. By Essanelle Salons.

HOLIDAY HAIRCARE

Permed hair needs extra protection from the drying effects of sun, salt, chlorine and wind. Use plenty of conditioner and rinse your hair after swimming. Curl revitalizers help by putting moisture back and keeping curls bouncy. Photograph courtesy of Bain de Terre Spa Therapy.

More damage can be done to the hair during a two-week holiday in the sun than the damage accrued during the rest of the year. The ultraviolet rays, or radiation, (UVRs) from sunlight that can cause damage to the skin can also have an adverse affect on the hair, depleting the natural oils and removing moisture. Strong winds whip unprotected hair into a tangle, causing breakage and split ends. Chlorinated and salt water cause colour fading and result in drooping perms.

Permed and coloured hair, weakened by chemicals, lose moisture at a faster rate than untreated hair. White hair is particularly susceptible to the effects of the sun because it has lost its natural pigmentation (melanin), which helps to filter out harmful UVRs to some degree.

OUT IN THE MIDDAY SUN

Protecting the hair from the sun's harmful rays makes as much sense as protecting the skin. Wear a hat or a scarf on the beach, or use a sun protective spray to shield the hair from the sun's harmful rays. After a swim, rinse the salt or chlorinated water thoroughly from the hair using plenty of fresh, clean water. If fresh water is not available take some with you in an empty soft drinks bottle or use bottled water.

Sunscreen gels are available for the hair and these offer a good deal of protection. Comb the gel through your hair and leave on all day. Remember to reapply the gel after swimming. Alternatively, use a leave-in conditioner, choosing one that protects the hair against UVRs.

On windy or blustery days, keep long hair tied back to prevent tangles. Long hair can also be braided when it is wet and the braid left in all day. When evening comes and you undo the braids you will have a cascade of rippling, Pre-Raphaelite curls.

If your hair does get tangled by the wind, untangle it gently by using a

Above: Slick short hair back with gel. Leave the gel in all day, then rinse out and style your hair in the evening. Photograph courtesy of Bain de Terre Spa Therapy.

BEFORE YOU GO

❍ Any hair colouring you are planning should be done at least one week prior to your holiday. This will allow the colour to "soften" and allow time for some intensive conditioning on any dry ends.

❍ If you want to have a perm before your holiday, book the appointment at least three weeks before departure to allow your hair to settle. You will also have the opportunity to learn how best to manage your new style and help overcome any dryness.

❍ Remember to pack all your holiday hair needs - your favourite shampoos, conditioners and styling products. And pack a selection of scarves and hair accessories. You will have more time to experiment on holiday.

❍ If possible take a travel dryer with dual voltage, and remember to pack an adaptor.

❍ Gas-powered stylers are convenient for holidays but remember they must be carried in the hold of the aircraft, not in your hand luggage. Refill cylinders are not allowed on aeroplanes, so fit a new cartridge before you go.

❍ Soft, bendy rollers are a good alternative to heated ones – they are also kinder to the hair.

❍ Have a trim before you go, but not a new style, as you won't want to worry about coping with a new look. Whatever you do, don't be tempted to have your hair cut abroad. Wait until you are back home and can visit your regular stylist.

Above: When the sun sets, apply mousse to straightened hair and sleek back behind the ears, flicking the ends up. Then leave to dry naturally. By Jon Pereira-Santos, Montage Hair Company, Windsor, England. Photography Suzy Corby.

Left: Breezy beach days whip the hair into a tangle. Take time to remove knots and snarls with a wide-toothed comb. Longer hair can be braided or knotted into a neat bun at the nape to keep it in place and prevent damage. Photograph courtesy of Silvikrin.

Top: After swimming, rinse the hair in clean, clear water and comb through with a wide-toothed comb. Use a sun-protective gel with a UVR filter for maximum care. By Daniel Galvin, London.

Above: To keep the hair in place, clasp it into a pretty slide (barrette). Colourful accessories are great for the beach; take a selection to mix and match with your swimwear. By Daniel Galvin, London.

Opposite. To get separation on long curls, mix a little conditioner with water and use a spray to mist the solution on to the hair. Scrunch the hair with your hands to create a casual look. Photograph courtesy of Bain de Terre Spa Therapy.

Opposite below: Pin fresh flowers in your hair for an alluring, feminine after-sun style. By Joseph and Jane Harling, Avon, England.

wide-toothed comb and work from the ends of the hair up towards the roots.

Keep your head and hair protected, even when you are away from the beach. Wear a sunhat when shopping or sightseeing, especially at midday. When the sun sets, shampoo and condition your hair and, if possible, let it dry naturally. Leave heat styling for those special nights out.

WINTER HAIRCARE

During the winter, and particularly on a winter break, your hair will be exposed to damaging conditions, such as harsh, biting winds and the drying effects of low temperatures and central heating. Central heating draws moisture from the hair and scalp, which causes static. Extreme cold makes the hair brittle and dry, and wet weather spells disaster for a style, making curly hair frizz and straight hair limp.

Above left: Long hair that is lightly layered gives lift on the crown and movement in the ends. For this look, rough-dry the hair and mist with styling lotion before setting on large rollers. When the hair is completely dry, lightly brush through to create soft waves and curls. By Taylor Ferguson, Glasgow, Scotland.

Above: Short, naturally curly hair can be given a pretty style by drying it with a small round brush and working the hair upwards. By Andrew Collinge, Liverpool and Harrods, London. Photography Iain Philpott.

These effects can be counteracted with a few simple measures. To reduce the drying effects of central heating, place large bowls of water near the radiators or use humidifiers. Use a more intensive conditioner on your hair in the winter to combat dryness caused by cold. In damp weather, apply a mousse, gel or hairspray; they are invaluable for keeping a style in place and giving some degree of protection.

ON THE PISTE

❍ The sun's rays are intensified by reflection from the snow, so hair needs extra protection in the form of a hair sunscreen.
❍ Wind, blasts of snow, and sunshine are a damaging combination for hair, so wear a hat whenever possible.
❍ In freezing temperatures, hair picks up static electricity, making it flyaway and unmanageable. Calm the static by spraying your brush with hairspray before brushing your hair.
❍ With sudden temperature changes – from icy cold slopes to a warm hotel – and constantly changing headgear your hair may need daily shampooing. Use a mild shampoo and light conditioner.

COLOURING AND BLEACHING

Hair colorants have never been technically better; nowadays it is a simple matter to add a temporary tone and gloss to the hair or make a more permanent change. And there is a wide variety of home colouring products from which to choose.

THE CHOICE

Temporary colours are usually water-based and are applied to shampooed, wet hair. They work by coating the outside, or cuticle layer, of the hair. The colour washes away in the next shampoo. Temporary colours are good

---

FACT FILE

❍ Colouring swells the hair shaft, making fine hair appear thicker.
❍ Because colour changes the porosity of the hair it can help combat greasiness.
❍ Rich tones reflect more light and give hair a thicker appearance.
❍ Highlights give fine hair extra texture and break up the heaviness of very thick hair.
❍ Too light a hair colour can make the hair appear thinner.

---

for a quick, but fleeting, change or for counteracting discoloration in blonde or white hair. Colour setting lotions combine a colour that washes out, with a strong setting lotion. They are similar to temporary colours and are perfect for adding tone to grey, white, or bleached hair.

Semi-permanent colours give a more noticeable effect that lasts for six to eight shampoos. They can only add, enrich, or darken hair colour, they cannot make it any lighter. Semi-permanent colours penetrate the cuticle and coat the outer edge of the cortex (the inner layer of the hair). The colour fades gradually and is ideal for those who want to experiment, but don't want to commit themselves to a more permanent change.

Longer-lasting, semi-permanent colours remain in the hair for 12–20 shampoos and are perfect for blending in the first grey hairs. The colour penetrates even deeper into the cortex than in semi-permanent colours. This type is perfect for a more lasting change.

Permanent colours lighten or darken, and effectively cover white. The colour enters the cortex during the development time (around 30 minutes) after which oxygen in the developer swells the pigments in the colorant, and holds them in. The roots may need retouching every six weeks. When retouching, it is important to colour only the new hair growth. If the new colour overlaps previously treated hair, there will be a build-up of colour from the mid-lengths to the ends, which will make the hair more porous.

The model's fine hair was made to look thicker by working fine highlights of different tonal values throughout the hair. The feather cut was then styled forward and blow-dried into shape. A little wax was rubbed between the palms of the hands and applied to the hair with the fingertips to give further definition. By Nicky Clarke, London.

Below: Ash-blonde hair was tapered at the sides so that it feathered on to the face. Fine textured hair like this needs gentle styling to maintain it in good condition, especially after colouring, so regular conditioning treatments are essential. By Steven Carey, London.

Above: These copper tones were achieved by applying a permanent tint; the volume of hair was then increased by using a hot-air brush to style the hair away from the face. You can get the same effect by working on one section of the hair at a time. Finish with firm-hold hairspray. Photograph courtesy of BaByliss.

Above: Here, reddish hues were created with a longer-lasting, semi-permanent colour that added deep tones and luminosity. The hair was blow-dried straight, pointing the nozzle of the dryer downwards in order to polish and encourage the shine. By Yosh Toya, San Francisco. Photography Gen.

Above: Russet tones were further emphasized by weaving a few lighter colours into the front hair. The hair was blow-dried with styling gel to get lift at the roots. By Daniel Galvin, London.

Left: The model's hair was lightened to achieve this soft shade of blonde. Remember, only lift your hair colour by one or two shades and don't forget that the roots will need retouching regularly. For this style, the hair was graduated and blow-dried into shape. By Daniel Galvin, London.

A variety of herbs and other plants have been used in the past to colour hair, and many of them have remained popular to this day. The natural dyes provide a semi-permanent colour, although the results that can be achieved will vary. They depend on the quality of the raw ingredients combined with the natural colour of the hair and how porous it is. Many top hairdressers mix their own vegetable dyes using a wide range of ingredients, as well as using commercial colours. By Daniel Galvin, London.

NATURAL COLOURING – HENNA

Vegetable colorants such as henna and camomile have been used since ancient times to colour hair, and henna was particularly popular with the Ancient Egyptians. Although henna is the most widely used natural dye, others can be extracted from a wide variety of plants, including marigold petals, cloves, rhubarb stalks and even tea leaves. Natural dyes work in much the same way as semi-permanent colorants by staining the outside of the hair. However, results are variable and a residue is often left behind, making further colouring with permanent tints or bleaches inadvisable.

Henna enhances natural highlights, making colour appear richer. It is available today as a powder, which is mixed with water to form a paste. The colour fades gradually, but frequent applications will give a stronger, longer-lasting effect. The result that is achieved when using henna depends on the natural colour of the hair. On brunette or black hair it produces a lovely reddish glow, while lighter hair becomes a beautiful titian. Henna will not lighten, and it is not suitable for use on blonde hair. On hair that is more than 20 per cent grey, white, tinted, bleached or highlighted, the resultant colour will be orange.

The longer the henna is left on the hair, the more intense the result. Timings vary from one to two hours, but some Indian women leave henna on the hair for 24 hours, anointing their heads with oil to keep the paste supple.

The condition of the hair being treated is another factor that affects the intensity. The ends of long hair are always slightly lighter than the roots because they are more exposed to the sun, and henna will emphasize this effect. The resulting colour will be darker on the roots to the mid-lengths and more vibrant from the mid-lengths to the ends.

It is always wise to test the henna you intend to use on a few loose hairs (the ones in your hairbrush will do),

noting the length of time it takes to produce the result you want.

Neutral henna can be used to add gloss and lustre to the hair without adding any colour. Mix the henna with water to a stiff paste. Stir in an egg yolk for extra conditioning, plus a little milk, which will help to keep the paste pliable. Apply to the hair and leave for an hour before rinsing thoroughly. Repeat every two to three months.

CAMOMILE

Camomile has a gentle, lightening effect on hair and is good for sun-streaking blonde and light brown hair. However, it takes several applications and a good deal of time to produce the desired effect. The advantage of camomile over chemical bleach is that it never gives a brassy or yellow tone. Best for blonde hair, it will also gently lighten red.

To make a camomile rinse for use after each shampoo, place 30 ml/2 tbsp

Above: Brunettes are very suitable candidates for having their hair coloured. Their hair can be considerably enriched and enhanced with a henna, which will produce brilliant depths and tones. By Wella Living Colours.

Above right: These vibrant, red tones were achieved using a mixture of vegetable dyes and by working highlights of different tones through the hair. The hair was then styled by blow-drying. By Daniel Galvin, London.

of dried camomile flowers in 600 ml/ 1 pint of boiling water. Simmer for 15 minutes, strain and cool before use.

To obtain more positive results add 150 g/5 oz/1 cup of dried camomile flowers to 300 ml/½ pint of boiling water and leave to steep for 15 minutes. Cool, simmer and strain. Add the juice of a fresh lemon plus 30 ml/2 tbsp of a rich cream conditioner. Comb through the hair and leave to dry – in the sun, if possible. Finally, shampoo and condition your hair as usual.

DOS AND DON'TS

○ Do rinse henna paste thoroughly, or the hair and scalp will feel gritty.
○ Don't expose hennaed hair to strong sunlight and always rinse salt and chlorine from the hair immediately after swimming.
○ Do use a henna shampoo between colour applications to enhance the tone.
○ Don't use shampoos and conditioners containing henna on blonde hair, grey hair, or hair that has been chemically treated.
○ Do use the same type of henna product each time you apply henna.
○ Don't use compound henna (one that has had metallic salts added); it can cause long-term hair colouring problems.

CHOOSING A NEW COLOUR

When choosing a colour, a basic rule is to keep to one or two shades at each side of your original tone. It is probably best to try a temporary colorant first; if you like the result you can choose a semi-permanent or permanent colorant next time. If you want to be a platinum blonde and you are a natural brunette, you should seek the advice of a professional hairdresser.

There are two important points to remember when considering a colour change. First, only have a colour change if your hair is in good condition; dry, porous hair absorbs colour too rapidly, leading to a patchy result. Second, your make-up may need changing to suit your new colour.

SPECIAL TECHNIQUES

Hairdressers have devised an array of colouring methods to create different effects. These include:

Flying colours, in which a combination of colours is applied with combs and brushes to the middle lengths and tips of the hair.

Highlights(lowlights), where fine strands of hair are tinted or bleached lighter or darker, or colour is added, just to give varying tones throughout the hair. This technique is sometimes called frosting or shimmering, particularly when bleach is used to give an overall lighter effect.

Slices, a technique in which assorted colours are applied through the hair to emphasize a cut and show movement.

COVERING WHITE HAIR

If you just want to cover a few white hairs, use a temporary or semi-permanent colour that will last for six to eight weeks. Choose one that is similar to your natural colour. If the hair is brown, applying a warm brown colour will pick out the white areas and give lighter chestnut highlights. Alternatively, henna will give a glossy finish, and at the same time produce stunning red highlights. For salt and pepper hair – hair with a

mixed amount of white with the natural colour – try a longer-lasting, semi-permanent colour. These last for up to 20 shampoos and also add shine.

When hair is completely white, it can be covered with a permanent tint, but with this type of colorant it is necessary to update the colour every four to six weeks, a fact that should be taken into consideration before choosing this option. Those who prefer to stay with their natural shade of white can improve on the colour by using toning shampoos, conditioners and styling products, which will remove any brassiness and add beautiful silvery tones.

CARING FOR COLOURED HAIR

Chlorinated and salt water, perspiration, and the weather all conspire to fade coloured hair, particularly red hair. However, special products are available that will help counteract fading, such as those containing ultraviolet filters that protect coloured hair from the effects of the sun. Other protective measures include rinsing the hair after swimming and using a shampoo designed for coloured hair, followed by a separate conditioner. Gently blot the hair after shampooing – never rub it vigorously as this ruffles the cuticle and can result in colour "escaping". Finally, use an intensive conditioning treatment at least once a month.

BLEACHING

Strictly speaking, anything that lightens the hair, bleaches it, but in the present context bleaching refers specifically to any treatment that removes colour from the hair – rather than adding colour, which is the purpose of permanent colorants. There are several different types of bleach on the market and they range from the mild brighteners that lift hair colour a couple of shades, to the more powerful mixes that completely strip hair of its natural colour.

Bleaching is quite a difficult process to do and is best left to a professional

Left: There is a wide range of natural tones to choose from when you are looking for a new hair colour.

Above: The alternative is to opt for more vibrant fashion shades. Colour swatches courtesy of L'Oréal Coiffure.

hairdresser. If misused it can be very harsh and drying on the hair. To get the best results, make sure your hair is in optimum condition prior to bleaching. Once the hair has been bleached, regular intensive conditioning treatments are essential.

COLOUR CORRECTION

If you have been colouring your hair for some time and want to go back to your natural colour and tone, consult a professional hairdresser. Hair that has been tinted darker than its normal shade will have to be colour-stripped with a bleach bath, until the desired colour is achieved. Hair that has been bleached or highlighted will need to be re-pigmented and then tinted to match the original colour. For best results, all these processes must be carried out in a salon where the technicians have access to a variety of specialist products.

HELPFUL HINTS FOR HOME HAIR COLOURING

Always read the directions supplied with the product before you start, and follow them precisely. Make sure you do a strand and skin sensitivity test, as detailed in the directions.

If you are retouching the roots of tinted or bleached hair, apply new colour to the regrowth area only. Any overlap will result in uneven colour and porosity, which, in turn, will adversely affect the condition of your hair.

Don't colour your hair at home if the hair is split or visibly damaged, or if you have used bleach or any type of henna; you must allow previously treated hair to grow out before applying new colour. Avoid colouring your hair if you are taking prescribed drugs, as the chemical balance of your hair can alter. Check with your family doctor first.

If your hair has been permed, consult a hairdresser before using a hair colorant. And if you are in any doubt about using a colour, always check with the manufacturer or consult a professional hair colourist.

FACT FILE

In the Middle Ages saffron and a mixture of sulphur, alum and honey were used for bleaching and colouring hair. These concoctions were not always safe, however, and in 1562 a certain Dr Marinello from Modena, Italy, wrote a treatise warning of the possible and undesirable consequences of bleaching the hair. He warned: "The scalp could be seriously damaged and the hair be destroyed at the roots and fall out."

Top and above: Burnished titian red tones give one of the most effective results when applied to natural brown hair. However, reddish hues are particularly prone to fade, so coloured hair should be protected from the sun. Specialist shampoos and conditioners should be used to help maintain colour. Photographs: top, Mark Hill for Wella; above, Zotos.

PERMANENT SOLUTIONS

Making straight hair curly is not a new idea. Women in Ancient Egypt coated their hair in mud, wound it around wooden rods and then used the heat from the sun to create the curls.

Waves that won't wash out are a more recent innovation. Modern perms were pioneered by A.F. Willat, who invented the cold permanent wave technique in 1934. Since then, improved formulations and ever more sophisticated techniques have made perms the most versatile styling option in hairdressing.

HOW THEY WORK

Perms work by breaking down inner structures (links) in your hair and re-forming them around a curler to give a new shape. Hair should be washed prior to perming as this causes the scales on the cuticles to rise gently, allowing the perming lotion to enter the hair shaft more quickly. The perming lotion alters the keratin and breaks down the sulphur bonds that link the fibre-like cells together in the inner layers of each hair. When these fibres have become loose, they can be formed into a new shape when the hair is stretched over a curler or a perming rod.

Once the curlers or rods are in place, more lotion is applied and the perm is left to develop to fix the new shape. The development time can vary according to the condition and texture of the hair. When the development is complete, the changed links in the hair are re-formed into their new shape by the application of a second chemical known as the neutralizer. The neutralizer contains an oxidizing agent that is effectively responsible for closing up the broken links and producing the wave or curl – permanently.

Specialist formulations enable your hairdresser to perm long hair while maintaining it in optimum condition. Here the hair was wound on to large rods to achieve a soft curl formation. Photograph courtesy of Clynol.

The type of curl that is produced depends on a number of factors. The size of the curler is perhaps the most important as this determines the size of the curl. Generally speaking, the smaller the curler the smaller and therefore tighter the curl, whereas medium to large curlers tend to give a much looser effect. The strength of lotion used can also make a difference, as can the texture and type of hair. Hair in good condition takes a perm much better than hair in poor condition, and fine hair curls more easily than coarse hair.

After a perm it takes 48 hours for the keratin in the hair to harden naturally. During this time the hair is vulnerable to damage and must be treated with care. Resist shampooing, brushing, vigorous combing, blow-drying or setting, any of which may cause the perm to drop.

Once hair has been permed it remains curly and shaped the way it has been formed, although new growth will be straight. As time goes by, the curl can soften, and if the hair is long, its weight may make the curl and the wave appear much looser.

HOME VERSUS SALON

Perming is such a delicate operation that many women prefer to leave it in the hands of experienced, professional hairdressers. The advantages of having hair permed in a salon are several. The hair is first analysed to see whether it is in a fit condition to take a perm; coloured, out-of-condition, or over-processed hair may not be suitable. With a professional perm, there is also a greater choice in the type of curl – different strengths of lotion and different winding techniques all give a range of curls that are not available in home perms.

Right: The model's thick hair was given a volume perm in order to produce a stunning style with the fullest look possible. By Kevin Murphy International for Clynol. Photography Martin Evening.

Above: Spiral perming gives a ringlet effect on long hair. It is important with hair of this length to re-perm only at the roots when the hair grows, or you may cause damage to previously permed hair. By Terence Renati, London and Melbourne.

POST PERM TIPS

❍ Don't wash newly permed hair for 48 hours after processing as any stress can cause curls to relax.
❍ Use shampoos and conditioners formulated for permed hair. They help retain the correct moisture balance and prolong the perm.
❍ Always use a wide-toothed comb and work from the ends upwards. Never brush the hair.
❍ Blot wet hair dry before styling, to prevent stretching.
❍ Avoid using too much heat on permed hair. If possible, wash, condition and leave to dry naturally.
❍ If your perm has lost its bounce, mist with water or try a curl reviver. These are designed to put instant volume and bounce into permed hair. They are also ideal for eliminating frizziness on naturally curly hair.
❍ Expect your perm to last three to six months, depending on the technique and lotion used.

HOME RULES

If you do use a perm at home, it is essential that you read and follow the instructions supplied with the product. Remember to do a test curl to check whether your hair is suitable, and check to make certain you have enough curlers. You will probably want to enlist the help of a friend, as it's impossible to curl the back sections of your own hair properly, so you'll need a helping hand.

Timing is crucial – don't be tempted to remove the lotion before the time given or leave it on longer than directed.

Above: Short, straight hair was root permed and then blow-dried into place. By Paul Falltrick, Falltricks, for Clynol.

DON'T DO IT YOURSELF IF...

○ your hair is very dry or damaged.
○ you have bleached or highlighted your hair: it may be too fragile. If in doubt, check with your hairdresser.
○ the traces of an old perm still remain in your hair.
○ you suffer from a scalp disorder such as eczema or have broken, irritated skin.

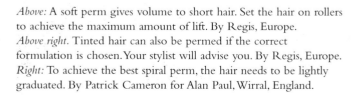

Above: A soft perm gives volume to short hair. Set the hair on rollers to achieve the maximum amount of lift. By Regis, Europe.
Above right. Tinted hair can also be permed if the correct formulation is chosen. Your stylist will advise you. By Regis, Europe.
Right: To achieve the best spiral perm, the hair needs to be lightly graduated. By Patrick Cameron for Alan Paul, Wirral, England.

SALON PERMS – THE CHOICES

Professional hairdressers can offer a number of different types of perm that are not available for home use:

Acid perms produce highly conditioned, flexible curls. They are ideally suited to hair that is fine, sensitive, fragile, damaged or tinted, as they have a mildly acidic action that minimizes the risk of hair damage.

Alkaline perms give strong, firm curl results on normal and resistant hair.

Exothermic perms give bouncy, resilient curls. "Exothermic" refers to the gentle heat that is produced by the chemical reaction that occurs when the lotion is mixed. The heat allows the lotion to penetrate the hair cuticle, conditioning and strengthening the hair from inside as the lotion moulds the hair into its new shape.

PERMING TECHNIQUES

Any of the above types of perm can be used with different techniques to produce a number of results.

Body perms are very soft, loose perms created by using large curlers, or sometimes rollers. The result is added volume with a hint of wave and movement, rather than curls.

Root perms add lift and volume to the root area only. They give height and fullness, and are therefore ideal for short hair that tends to go flat.

Pin curl perms give soft, natural waves and curls, which are achieved by perming small sections of hair that have been pinned into pre-formed curls.

Stack perms give curl and volume to one-length haircuts by means of different sized curlers. The hair on top of the head is left unpermed while the middle and ends have curl and movement.

Spiral perms create romantic spiral curls, an effect that is produced by winding the hair around special, long curlers. The mass of curls makes long hair look much thicker.

Spot perms give support only on the area to which they are applied. For example, if the hair needs lift the perm is applied just on the crown. They can also be used on the fringe (bangs) or side areas around the face.

Weave perms involve perming certain sections of hair and leaving the rest straight to give a mixture of texture and natural-looking body and bounce, particularly on areas around the face such as the fringe (bangs).

REGROWTH PROBLEM

When a perm is growing out, the areas of new growth can be permed if a barrier is created between old and new growth. The barrier can be a special cream or a plastic protector, both of which effectively prevent the perming lotion and neutralizer from touching previously permed areas.

There are also products that facilitate re-perming an entire length of hair without damaging the structure. These more complex solutions are only available from salons.

To keep a full perm looking its best, shampoo, apply mousse, then blow-dry using a diffuser, or set the hair on rollers. By L'Oréal.

BLACK HAIR

One of the most effective ways of styling very curly hair is to crop it close and short. With this type of cut you just need to shampoo, condition and finish it with soft wax. By Macmillan, London.

Black hair is fragile, yet difficult to control, therefore it needs specialist care and pampering if it is to look its best.

This type of hair is almost always curly, although the degree of wave varies enormously. As a general rule, black hair is brittle and has a tendency to split and break. This is because the sebaceous glands produce insufficient sebum to moisturize the hair. In addition, because the hair is tightly curled, the sebum is unable to travel downwards to condition it naturally. If the curl forms kinks, this makes the hair thinner, and therefore weaker, at each bend.

Other types of black hair can be very fine, making it difficult to style and hold a set.

To treat excessive dryness, choose a specialist formulation that replaces the natural oils lacking in black hair. If the product is massaged in daily, or whenever necessary, the hair will become more manageable with improved condition and shine. It is also important to deep condition the hair regularly.

STRAIGHTENING THE HAIR

Straightening, or relaxing, is in fact perming in reverse. A hair straightener, also known as a chemical relaxer, is combed or worked through the hair to change the structure and to straighten it. The result is permanent, only disappearing as the hair grows. Chemical relaxers come in different strengths to suit different hair textures and styles.

Before: Long, thick natural hair can be totally transformed with the technique known as weaving. To do this the hair is corn-row braided and then weaves are sewn on to the braided base.

Hair that has been straightened is blow-dried using a vent brush. Straightening irons could also be used to achieve a similarly smooth effect. By Richard M.F. Mendleson, David's Hair Designers, Maryland, USA.

PROFESSIONAL TIP

Hair needs to be strong and healthy to take any type of chemical treatment. To check hair strength and natural elasticity, pluck out a hair and hold it firmly between the fingers of both hands, then pull gently. If the hair breaks with hardly any stretching, it is weak and in poor condition, in which case all chemical treatments should be avoided.

After: Once the weave has been sewn into place, the new hair is cut and styled as desired. The result of all this work is a completely different look. By Eugene, Xtension Masters, London.

They are particularly effective on longer styles as the weight of the hair helps to maintain the straightened look. If you do this at home get advice first, and make sure you use high-quality, branded products and follow the instructions precisely to get the best results.

DEMI PERMING

Very curly hair can also be tamed by perming. This enables tight curls to be replaced by larger, looser ones. Demi-perms are good for short hair, giving a more controlled, manageable shape; on long hair they produce a softer, bouncier look. The more advanced perms involve softening the hair by weaving it on to rollers and then neutralizing it so that the curls are permanently set into their new shape.

To prevent frizziness and maintain the definition of curls, special lotions called curl activators and moisturizing sprays can be used to revive and preserve the formation of curls.

As with all chemical treatments, relaxing and perming can be potentially harmful to the hair, removing natural moisture and leaving hair in a weakened state. For this reason it is advisable to get skilled professional help and advice.

HOT COMBS

Before chemical relaxers became available the most popular hair straightening method was "hot pressing". This involved putting a pre-heated iron comb through the hair to loosen the curls. Up-to-date versions, called thermal texturizers, are electric pressing combs, which work in a similar way to loosen and soften very curly hair.

COLOUR OPTIONS

Because of its natural dryness and porosity, black hair should be coloured with caution, preferably by a professional hairdresser. If the hair has been straightened, relaxed or permed, it may be too weak to colour successfully.

Techniques such as highlighting, lowlighting, or tipping the ends are best for this type of hair.

SPECIAL PROBLEMS

Traction hair loss is caused by braiding or weaving hair too tightly. If the hair is pulled too forcibly too often, it will disrupt the hair follicles, cause scar tissue to form and, ultimately, hair loss. To help prevent this, avoid braiding or pulling the hair into tight braids. Similar problems can also result from misusing perming and relaxing chemicals.

After straightening or relaxing, black hair can be styled smooth using blow-drying techniques. *Left:* The hair has been smoothed into curls. *Centre:* Here it has been flicked up at the ends and the fringe (bangs) curved. *Right:* For this style it was piled into soft curls and given a fuller fringe (bangs). By Richard M.F. Mendleson, David's Hair Designers, Maryland, USA.

KEEPING BLACK HAIR BEAUTIFUL

○ Use a wide-toothed Afro comb for curly hair and a natural bristle brush for relaxed hair. Combing will help spread the natural oils through the hair, making it look shinier and healthier. Use intensive pre-shampoo treatments.

○ Massage the scalp regularly to encourage oil production.

○ Shampoo as often as you feel necessary but only lather once, using a small amount of shampoo. Rinse thoroughly. Towel-blot, don't rub hair.

○ Once a month try a hot oil treatment, which will lubricate dry scalp conditions as well as moisturize brittle hair.

○ If you have a delicate fringe (bangs) or baby fine hair around the hairline (sometimes from breakage, sometimes an inherited trait), use a tiny round brush and a hairdryer to blend in this hair.

○ Gels are good for moulding black hair into shape; choose non-greasy formulas that give hair a healthy sheen.

○ If you use hot combs or curling tongs, make sure you shield the hair by using a protective product.

○ For extra hold and added shine, use a finishing spray.

○ Braided hair needs a softening shampoo that maintains the moisture balance and helps eliminate a dry scalp.

SUCCESSFUL STYLING

SUCCESSFUL STYLING MEANS CHOOSING A

HAIRSTYLE THAT SUITS YOUR LOOKS AND LIFESTYLE,

AND THEN LEARNING THE TECHNIQUES THAT WILL

ENSURE A PERFECT FINISH. TODAY,

THERE IS AN ENORMOUS RANGE OF GADGETS, HAIR

PRODUCTS AND HEATED STYLING EQUIPMENT AVAILABLE

TO THE GENERAL PUBLIC, ALL OF WHICH, USED

PROPERLY, CAN EFFECT WONDERFUL TRANSFORMATIONS.

THE TRICK IS TO KNOW WHAT TO USE AND WHEN TO USE

IT IN ORDER TO ACHIEVE THE DESIRED RESULTS.

HERE, WE SHOW YOU HOW.

CHOOSING A STYLE

Make the most of your looks by choosing a style that maximizes your best features. The first feature you should consider is your face shape – is it round, oval, square or long? If you are not sure what shape it is then the easiest way to find out is to scrape your hair back off your face. Stand squarely in front of a mirror and use a lipstick to trace the outline of your face on to the mirror. When you stand back you should be able to see into which of the following categories your face shape falls.

THE ROUND FACE

On the round face the distance between the forehead and the chin is about equal to the distance between the cheeks. Choose a style with a short fringe (bangs), which lengthens the face, and a short cut, which makes it look thinner. **Styles to avoid:** Curly styles, because they emphasize the roundness; very full, long hair or styles that are scraped right back off the face.

THE LONG FACE

The long face is characterized by a high forehead and long chin, and needs to be given the illusion of width. Soften the effect with short layers, or go for a bob with a fringe (bangs), which will create horizontal lines. Scrunch-dried or curly bobs balance a long face. **Styles to avoid:** Styles without fringes (bangs), and long, one-length cuts.

THE COMPLETE YOU

When choosing a new style you should also take into account your overall body shape. If you are a traditional pear-shape don't go for elfin styles; they will draw attention to the lower half of your body, making your hips look even wider. Petite women should avoid masses of very curly hair as this makes the head appear larger and out of proportion with the body.

THE SQUARE FACE

The square face is angular with a broad forehead and a square jawline. To make the best of this shape, choose a hairstyle with long layers, preferably one with soft waves or curls, as these create a softness that detracts from the hard lines. The hair should be parted at the side of the head and any fringe (bangs) combed away from the face. **Styles to avoid:** Severe geometric cuts – they will only emphasize squareness; long bobs with heavy fringes (bangs) ; severe styles in which the hair is scraped off the face and parted down the centre.

THE OVAL FACE

The oval face has wide cheekbones that taper down into a small, often pointed, chin, and up to a fairly narrow forehead. This is regarded by many experts as the perfect face shape. If your face is oval in shape then you are able to wear any hairstyle you choose.

IF YOU WEAR GLASSES...

Try to choose frames and a hairstyle that complement each other. Large spectacles could spoil a neat, feathery cut, and very fine frames could be overpowered by a large, voluminous style. Remember to take your glasses to the salon when having your hair restyled, so that your stylist can take their shape into consideration when deciding on the overall effect.

SPECIFIC PROBLEMS

❍ Prominent nose: incorporate softness into your style.
❍ Pointed chin: style hair with width at the jawline.
❍ Low forehead: choose a style with a wispy fringe (bangs), rather than one with a full fringe.
❍ High forehead: disguise with a fringe (bangs).
❍ Receding chin: select a style that comes just below chin level, with waves or curls.
❍ Uneven hairline: a fringe (bangs) should conceal this problem.

Left: A wispy fringe (bangs) stylishly disguises a low forehead. Hair by Sam McKnight for Silvikrin.
Above: A high forehead or uneven hairline can be hidden under a full fringe (bangs). Hair by Paul Falltrick. Photography Iain Philpott.
Below: Strong features benefit from a soft, full hairstyle. Hair by Jed Hamill, Graham Webb International for Clynol. Photography Ian Hooton.

STYLE GALLERY, SHORT HAIR

Short hair can be cut close,
cropped or layered in a
variety of styles.

Fine, straight hair was lightly layered and
cut close into the nape. A root perm
provided extra volume at the crown of
the head. The hair was then finger-dried
using a styling mousse. By Yosh Toya,
San Francisco. Photography Gen.

Naturally wavy hair was lightly layered
to encourage movement. A wet-look gel
was applied and the hair was combed
into soft waves and side curls, then left
to dry naturally. By Regis, Europe.
Photography John Swannell.

Naturally wavy hair was cut into a one-
length bob and taken behind the ears,
using wet-look gel to give definition
and accentuate the waves. By Regis,
Europe. Photography John Swannell.

Far left: Thick hair was feather-cut into layers, with slightly longer lengths left at the nape. The hair was highlighted and then blow-dried into shape using a styling brush. *Left:* For a different look the hair was combed down over the ears. By Regis Europe. Photography John Swannell.

Left: Fine hair was softly layered and given an application of mousse, then the hair was ruffle-dried with the fingers to create just a little lift at the roots. *Right:* The same haircut was blow-dried forwards using a styling brush. By Regis, Europe. Photography John Swannell.

Medium-textured hair was cut into face-framing layers. Mousse was applied from the roots to the ends, then the hair was blow-dried forwards, using the fingers to rake through the hair from the back to the front. By Paul Falltrick, Falltricks, Essex, England for Clynol. Photography Alistair Hughes.

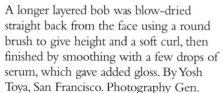

A longer layered bob was blow-dried straight back from the face using a round brush to give height and a soft curl, then finished by smoothing with a few drops of serum, which gave added gloss. By Yosh Toya, San Francisco. Photography Gen.

Medium-textured hair was cut into layers of the same length, then blow-dried using a strong-hold mousse to get lift, and finished with a mist of firm-hold hairspray. By Daniel Galvin, London.

A short, urchin cut is good for all hair textures. Highlights give extra interest and add thickness to finer hair. By Nicky Clarke, London. Photography Paul Cox.

A short, feathery cut was set off with a straight, cropped fringe (bangs). For this style, the hair can be either left to dry naturally, or blow-dried while ruffling with the fingers. By Anestis Kyprianou, Cobella, London, for Schwarzkopf. Photography Martin Evening.

Medium-textured hair was graduated to give this head-hugging cut. Mousse was applied from the roots to the ends, then the hair was blow-dried forwards from the crown. By Neville Daniel, London, for Lamaur.

Very curly, wiry hair was cropped close to the head, then dressed using just a little wax to give definition and separation. By Frank Hession, Dublin, Eire, for L'Oréal Coiffure.

This soft style is ideal for hair with more than a hint of natural wave; layering gives additional movement. After an application of a little mousse (styling gel would be equally suitable) the hair was left to dry naturally, occasionally running the fingers through to encourage curl. By Beverly Kyprianou, Cobella, London, for Schwarzkopf. Photography Martin Evening.

Thick hair was razor cut to give forward movement, then blow-dried for a few seconds with the dryer set on high heat, at the same time brushing in all directions to give extra movement. By John Frieda, London and New York.

A short cut was given extra interest by bleaching the hair honey-blonde. It was then blow-dried into shape and finished using wax to create separation. By Yosh Toya, San Francisco. Photography Gen.

One-length hair was parted at the side and slicked down with a wet-look gel to create this slick style. Pictures left to right by Joseph and Jane Harling, Avon, England. Photography Ruth Crafer.

Fine hair was softly layered and combed forwards. A little wax was rubbed between the palms and applied with the fingertips to strands of hair in order to achieve separation.

A thick, one-length bob was blow-dried very smooth from a side parting. The hair was misted with hairspray and smoothed with the hands to eliminate wisps.

Wispy, fine hair was given extra volume with a light perm, then blow-dried forwards. A semi-permanent colour gives this type of hair added depth.

Choppy layers give an uneven texture to this thick hair. The hair was blow-dried using mousse and a styling brush to create lift. By Alan Edwards for L'Oréal Coiffure.

A root perm helped to give lift at the crown for this short, layered look. Mousse was applied to give extra lift and the hair was blow-dried forwards from the crown. By Neville Daniel, London. Photography Will White.

Very straight hair was cut into a neat, face-framing shape, then blow-dried forwards. It was then finished with a mist of shine spray for added gloss. By Andrew Collinge, Liverpool and Harrods, London. Photography Iain Philpott.

Left: A short, layer cut was coloured copper and styled using gel before ruffle-drying with fingers to get lift and separation.
Right: For an alternative look, hair is smoothed at the front and backcombed on the crown. A little hairspray keeps hair in place. By Joseph and Jane Harling, Avon, England. Photography Barry Cook.

The hair was roller set and dried thoroughly. After removing the rollers, it was brushed through and backcombed at the roots to give volume. By Joseph and Jane Harling, Avon, England. Photography Iain Philpott.

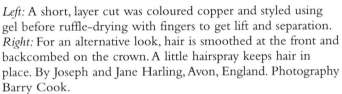

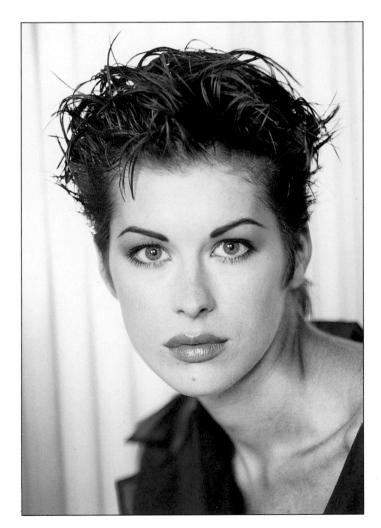

Left: A layer cut was styled using wet gel to create texture and movement. The hair was lifted at the roots with fingers to get height. By Joseph and Jane Harling, Avon, England. Photography Iain Philpott.

Right: Gel was used to slick back hair and give separation to a long fringe that is combed forward. By Joseph and Jane Harling, Avon, England. Photography Iain Philpott.

Right: High-lift bleach is best used on very short hair like this which will need regular intensive conditioning to keep it shiny. By Joseph and Jane Harling, Avon, England. Photography Iain Philpott.

A razored bob was highlighted to break up the texture. The hair was blow-dried forward using mousse and a vent brush and finished with a light mist of shine serum. By Imij for L'Oréal Professionnel.

The hair was blow-dried using a round bristle brush and misted with shine spray. By Tina Shaw, Dimensions, Sheffield, England, for Goldwell Hair Cosmetics. Photography Ian Lea.

Natural curls were scrunch-dried then a few drops of serum were worked into the ends of the hair to give definition. By Storm, Southampton, England, for L'Oréal Professionnel.

A layered cut was set on heated rollers which were allowed to cool completely before being removed. The hair was then brushed with a vent brush with a little backcombing at the roots for extra height. By Joseph and Jane Harling, Avon, England. Photography Barry Cook.

Right: A few chunky highlights at the front of the hair give extra interest to a short crop. By Tina Shaw, Dimensions, Sheffield, England, for Goldwell Hair Cosmetics. Photography Ian Lea.

A choppy cut was rough-dried then sections straightened using flat irons. Bold streaks of blonde add interest to this cut. By Barbara Daley for L'Oréal Professionel.

A lightly layered blonde crop was blow-dried forward from the crown using mousse and a styling brush. Wax was worked through to create texture. By Joseph and Jane Harling, Avon, England. Photography Barry Cook.

A short crop was coloured with a permanent copper tint and gel set, then simply ruffled with fingers to achieve separation. By Joseph and Jane Harling, Avon, England. Photography Iain Philpott.

The hair was slicked behind the ears with strong gel. The crown hair was backcombed at the roots and misted with strong-hold hairspray. By Joseph and Jane Harling, Avon, England. Photography Barry Cook.

A one-length, straight bob was dried using mousse and a medium-sized, round bristle brush to achieve texture. By Sharon Malcolm, Hair Traffic, Belfast, N. Ireland.

Fine, naturally curly hair was wet set using gel which was worked into the roots by lifting the hair, then left to dry naturally. By Joseph and Jane Harling, Avon, England. Photography Iain Philpott.

A really short crop was brilliantly coloured with shades of copper and burgundy. The hair was styled using a small, round bristle brush and finished with strong-hold hairspray. By Sharon Malcolm, Hair Traffic, Belfast, N. Ireland.

Strong blonde and copper lights give interest to this short cut. It was styled using a vent brush to get height on the crown and the ends were flicked out using a small round brush. By Sharon Malcolm, Hair Traffic, Belfast, N. Ireland.

Fine hair was coloured strawberry blonde with a permanent tint which, as well as colouring, gives hair more body. Styled by blow-drying forward with a vent brush. By Nicky Oliver, Manchester, England, for Schwarzkopf. Photography Alan Pickering.

One-length bobs are great for straight or slightly wavy hair. The hair was blow-dried with mousse or gel using a vent brush and pointing the barrel of the dryer downwards for maximum smoothness. By Robert Bell, Woodford Green, Essex, England.

A strong copper permanent colour sets off this simple bob which was cut with a high fringe to frame the face. By Edward Hemmings, Alan d, London.

A one-length, short bob was tapered at the back to fit neatly into the nape. It was dried using a styling brush to smooth hair flat and sleek. By Robert Bell, Woodford Green, Essex, England.

A heavy fringe (bangs) is perfect with a jaw-length bob. The hair was coloured with shades of burgundy-red permanent colour which gives a long-lasting result. By Edward Hemmings, Alan d, London.

Thick hair was razor cut to fall into a neat cap shape. The hair was left to dry naturally and finished with just a little spray shine worked through with the fingers. By Robert Bell, Woodford Green, Essex, England.

Two-tone colour along the parting gives a one-length bob a fresh look. Blow-dried straight with a styling brush. By Edward Hemmings, Alan d, London.

Fine hair was given a new look with bold red and gold lights. Blow-dried smooth using a vent brush. By Jonathan Woodward, Greta Kahn, London.

A high-lift tint gives the ultimate blondness to this short, choppy cut. Ruffle-dried with fingers, using wax. By Tracie Cant and Ray Wilson for Labothene Academy, Pforzheim, Germany.

Hair was cut very short and misted all over with liquid gel. Blast-dried, working up from the roots for height. By Nicky Oliver, Manchester, England, for Schwarzkopf.

A textured, one-length bob was bleached with a high-lift tint. To keep hair shiny use a leave-in conditioner and allow hair to dry naturally, finishing with a little wax for added lustre. By Wendy Jones and Vince Barry, The Martin Cox Salon, Sutton Coldfield, England. Photography Martin Cox.

Blonde ends and dark roots give a great look for short hair. The hair was blast-dried with gel, lifting hair at the roots to achieve height. By Nicky Oliver, Manchester, England, for Schwarzkopf. Photography Alan Pickering.

The hair was blast-dried with spray gel to get lots of lift for this fun look. By Nicky Oliver, Manchester, England, for Schwarzkopf. Photography Alan Pickering.

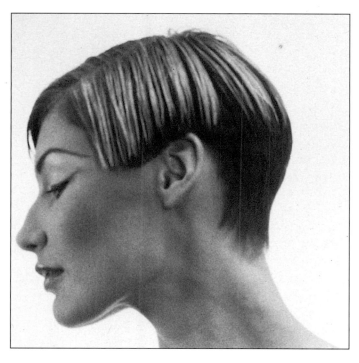

Variations on the bob were smoothed flat using the nozzle attachment on the hairdryer and polished with a mist of shine spray. By Tracie Cant and Ray Wilson for Labothene Academy, Pforzheim, Germany.

Longer lengths on top contrast with the nape hair cut really short. By Wendy Jones and Vince Barry, The Martin Cox Salon, Sutton Coldfield, England.

Thick hair was cut into using a technique called chipping, which makes hair easy to style. A little mousse was applied and ruffle-dried with fingers. Finished with a little wax, warmed between palms, and worked through the hair. By Tracie Cant and Ray Wilson for Labothene Academy, Pforzheim, Germany.

Fine hair was cut so it flicks out to give interest to a short cut. An ebony, semi-permanent rinse adds depth to the style. By Tracie Cant and Ray Wilson for Labothene Academy, Pforzheim, Germany.

Very fine hair looks good cut short and simply dried forward from the crown. Spray shine adds a touch of lustre and helps reflect light. By Tracie Cant and Ray Wilson for Labothene Academy, Pforzheim, Germany.

A short cut was ruffle-dried with fingers and swept forward on to the face for this fresh look. By Tracie Cant and Ray Wilson for Labothene Academy, Pforzheim, Germany.

Fine hair can be given more texture by razor cutting and backcombing at the roots before ruffle-drying. By Sarah Hodge Hairdressing, Somerset and Devon, England. Photography Sanders Nicolson.

Thick hair was cut to fall forward and frame the face. The style can be left to dry naturally or diffuser-dried for speed. By Akin Konizi and The HOB Artistic Team, Hair on Broadway, Hertfordshire, Middlesex and London for Wella. Photography Chris Bishop.

A crop was dried using a small round bristle brush to achieve height at the crown and held in place with hairspray. By Akin Konizi and The HOB Artistic Team, Hair on Broadway, Hertfordshire, Middlesex and London for Wella. Photography Chris Bishop.

For a smoother cropped look, mousse was worked well into the roots and through the hair which was blow-dried flat to the head with a styling brush. By Akin Konizi and The HOB Artistic Team, Hair on Broadway, Hertfordshire, Middlesex and London for Wella. Photography Chris Bishop.

Asian hair can be fine and flyaway and is best blunt cut like this. The hair was smoothed with gel and left to dry naturally. By Edward Hemmings, Alan d, London, for Schwarzkopf.

The hair was cut short and root permed to give texture then styled with gel and left to dry naturally. By Barbara Daley, Barbara Daley Hair & Beauty, Liverpool, England, for L'Oréal Professionnel. Photography Chris Bishop.

The hair was blow-dried straight using liquid gel for added gloss then a section taken from the front and tonged to fall into soft curls. By Barbara Daley, Liverpool, England, for L'Oréal Professionnel. Photography Chris Bishop.

A one-length, blonde bob was blunt cut at the ends to encourage it to flick out. The hair was rough-dried then straightened using flat irons. By Ozzie Rizzo, Sanrizz, London. Photography Ozzie Rizzo.

A short-line bob was cut blunt then razored just on the ends to achieve a choppy finish. The hair was styled using cream to give smoothness. By Ozzie Rizzo, Sanrizz, London. Photography Ozzie Rizzo.

A choppy fringe (bangs) gives a new look to this very short crop. The hair was styled using a round bristle brush and gel. By Akin Konizi and The HOB Artistic Team, Hair on Broadway, Hertfordshire, Middlesex and London for Wella. Photography Chris Bishop.

The hair was cut into at random to give a really choppy, textured finish. Sections were smoothed with flat irons and held in place with spray gel or hard-to-hold hairspray. By Akin Konizi and The HOB Artistic Team, Hair on Broadway, Hertfordshire, Middlesex and London for Wella. Photography Chris Bishop.

The hair was coloured copper with random blonde highlights to give a lovely two-tone effect. It was blow-dried forward using a vent brush to give texture. By Akin Konizi and The HOB Artistic Team, Hair on Broadway, Hertfordshire, Middlesex and London for Wella. Photography Chris Bishop.

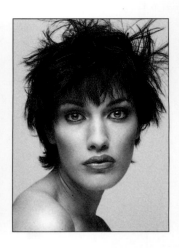

A short cut was styled by misting with strong-hold gel and blast-dried with the head held upside down to get maximum lift. Edward Hemmings, Alan d, London, for Schwarzkopf.

Burgundy and copper tones create a two-tone effect on a shaggy cut. The hair was blow-dried using mousse. By Akin Konizi and The HOB Artistic Team, Hair on Broadway, Hertfordshire, Middlesex and London for Wella.

Short, straight hair was gel set by combing flat to the head on the crown and lifting crown hair upwards using a comb. By Martine Finnegan, Natural Hair Company, Lisburn, N. Ireland.

Fine hair was razor cut to give it maximum volume. The hair was styled by applying gel then blast-dried with high heat to get a tousled finish. By Sarah Hodge Hairdressing, Somerset and Devon, England.

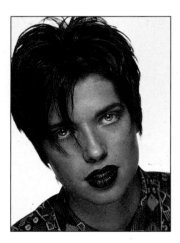

Root lift was achieved on a short cut by using a small, round bristle brush to lift hair at the roots, rolling hair over the brush to smooth out any kinks. By Nicky Oliver, Manchester, England, for Schwarzkopf. Photography Alan Pickering.

Medium-textured hair was cut into a short-line bob and smoothed with a bristle brush to give extra shine. By Nicky Oliver, Manchester, England, for Schwarzkopf. Photography Alan Pickering.

Naturally curly hair was cropped very short and wet-look gel applied. The hair was then ruffled with fingers and left to dry. By Martine Finnegan, Natural Hair Company, Lisburn, N. Ireland. Photography Rick Bond.

A short, blonde crop was cut to lie flat and smooth and a little mousse worked through the hair before drying. By Richard Ward and Roger Britnel, Richard Ward Hair & Beauty, London.

Fine hair was cut very short on the crown to form tufts, flatter at the sides with longer lengths left round the ears. The hair was ruffle-dried with mousse and finished with wax. By Johanna Cree, The Rainbow Room for Schwarzkopf.

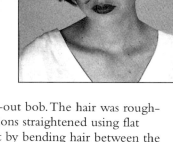

Above: Variations on the flicked-out bob. The hair was rough-dried, then gel applied and sections straightened using flat irons. The ends were turned out by bending hair between the plates of the irons, then held with hairspray. By Derek Preston, Klownz, Edinburgh, Scotland.

Left: A short, textured cut was given extra definition by razor cutting the front section. To style, wax was applied to the roots and the hair dried upside-down to give maximum lift. By Marc Griffiths and Stewart Mason, Marc Stewart, Essex, for Schwarzkopf. Photography Terence Renati.

The hair was cut into a jaw-length bob with heavy, razor-cut layers. To style, mousse and gel were applied and straightening irons used from root to tip to create shattered ends. By Tomy, Moga, London, for Schwarzkopf. Photography Terence Renati.

A graduated bob was cut longer at the front than the back so it falls around the face. The hair was blow-dried smooth using a large paddle brush. Any wispy ends were slicked into place by misting the hairbrush with styling spray and smoothing through outer layers of hair. By Nicky Oliver, Manchester, England.

Straight hair was blunt cut and simply dried with mousse and a paddle brush to give smoothness. By Richard Ward, Richard Ward Hair & Beauty, London.

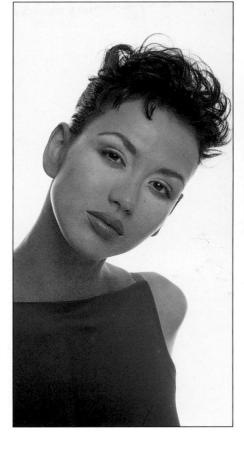

Above and right: The hair was graduated from the nape and softened at the sides to enhance the natural curl. The hair was styled by smoothing conditioning cream through from root to tip to define curls. Leave loose or slick back sides for a sophisticated style. By Lorraine Matthews and Sharon Brown, Jericho, Middlesex, England for Schwarzkopf.

A blonde bouffant was achieved by using heated rollers to set hair. The rollers were removed when completely cool, and the hair brushed into a bob using a bristle brush. By Martine Finnegan, the Natural Hair Company, Lisburn, N. Ireland.

The hair was coloured ebony-black to give drama to this bob. It was blow-dried smooth with a styling brush and finished with shine spray. By Terry Calvert, Clipso, Watford, Hemel Hempstead and St. Albans, England. Photography Martin Evening.

A short cut was given lift by root tonging all over, leaving ends to loop over and giving a brilliant new-look texture. By Terry Calvert, Clipso, Watford, Hemel Hempstead and St. Albans, England. Photography Martin Evening.

A short cut was slicked flat to the head with wet-look gel and finger-waved using a large styling comb. By Martine Finnegan, the Natural Hair Company, Lisburn, N. Ireland.

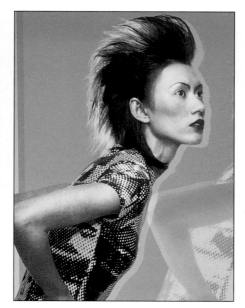

Thick, naturally wavy hair was quiffed (combed) back at the front using gel and the ends allowed to flick out on the crown. The sides were slicked behind the ears and smoothed into place. By Giovanni Ieronimo, Cutting Club, Cleethorpes, Lincolnshire, England. Photography Chris Bishop.

Gel was applied from the roots to the ends and worked well in before the hair was blast-dried with the head held forwards to achieve maximum height. By Terry Calvert, Clipso, Watford, Hemel Hempstead and St. Albans, England. Photography Martin Evening.

Short, fine hair was given texture by applying a wet-look gel and working through. The hair was combed into place and left to dry naturally. By Giovanni Ieronimo, Cutting Club, Cleethorpes, Lincolnshire, England. Photography Chris Bishop.

Straight, closely cropped hair was styled by using gel then blast-dried whilst combing hair upwards using a wide-toothed comb. By Ozzie Rizzo, Sanrizz, London. Photography Ozzie Rizzo.

Straight hair was cropped short and highlighted at the front then blast-dried with strong-hold mousse and finished by working wax through the ends. By Lara Johnson, Mumbles, Swansea, Wales. Photography David Fernandez.

A root perm gives fine hair body and makes it easier to style. Here the hair has been blow-dried straight back, while lifting at the roots. By Michael Aronberg, W1 Hair Design, Ilford, Essex, England. Photography Chris Bishop.

A textured short cut was misted with gel spray and diffuser-dried with the head held forward. Styling cream was worked through the ends to give separation. By Andrew Collinge, Liverpool and Harrods, London for Styling Solutions.

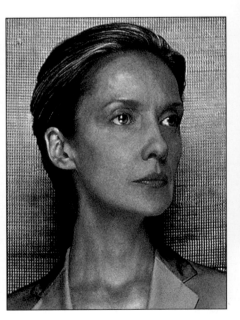

A one-length short crop was gelled back and combed straight with a wide-toothed comb. By Antoinette Beender, The Aveda Concept Salon, Harvey Nichols, London.

A short, layered look was styled using liquid gel to give fullness, then styling wax which was worked into the ends to give added texture. The hair was finished by allowing it to fall sexily over one eye. Hair by Andrew Collinge, Liverpool and Harrods, London, for Styling Solutions.

Above and right: Naturally curly hair was cut to maximize movement, then finger-dried using gel to give texture. For an alternative look, the hair was slicked back. By Martyn Maxey, Martyn Maxey Hairdressing, London.

Fine hair was razored so it flows on to the face. Longer pieces were left at the back to give a point of difference. The hair was blow-dried with a low heat and airflow for maximum smoothness. By Martyn Maxey, Martyn Maxey Hairdressing, London.

Left: Russet tones give depth and an incredible shine to this one-length classic bob. By Harry Boocock and Chris Horsman, The Hair Studio for Schwarzkopf.

Right: Bold copper highlights give added interest to this short cut. The hair was blow-dried forward using gel spray and finished with a mist of spray shine. By The Hair Studio for Schwarzkopf.

Medium-textured, straight hair was cut into a one-length bob. It was dried using mousse and a styling brush, switching to a round brush when the hair was nearly dry to turn ends under on to face. By Sharon Malcolm, Hair Traffic, Belfast, N. Ireland.

A curved bob is set off with a heavy, short fringe (bangs). A vegetable colour adds a deep shine and lustre. The hair was blow-dried with mousse and a styling brush to tip ends under. By Martyn Maxey, Martyn Maxey Hairdressing, London.

A choppy, modern cut was given a great look with slashes of blonde worked through. The hair was rough-dried and finished with styling cream. By Mark Smith, Staffords, The House That Hair Built, Leigh-on-Sea, Essex, England, for Yum Yum. Photography Dean Chalky.

A strawberry-blonde permanent tint gives this bob a deep shine and intense colour. The hair was blow-dried smooth using mousse and a paddle brush. By Sharon Malcolm, Hair Traffic, Belfast, N. Ireland.

A short crop is coloured brilliant copper. The hair was styled with mousse using a round bristle brush to dry hair a section at a time. By Sharon Malcolm, Hair Traffic, Belfast, N. Ireland.

Naturally curly hair was cut short and the curls smoothed out a little using a round bristle brush. By Sharon Malcolm, Hair Traffic, Belfast, N. Ireland.

Very short hair was first dried smooth at the front and high at the back, then, for an alternative look, one side was flicked out. By Studio One, Scotland.

An elfin cut on fine hair takes on a different dimension when bold streaks of blonde are woven through the front. The hair was blow-dried using mousse and a styling brush. By Sharon Malcolm, Hair Traffic, Belfast, N. Ireland.

A straight short cut was blow-dried smooth then a small piece on the crown clasped into a ponytail. By Sharon Malcolm, Hair Traffic, Belfast, N. Ireland.

An ebony-black rinse gives this choppy bob a deep colour. The hair was blow-dried with styling cream for maximum shimmer. By John Carne Artistic Team, Guildford, England.

A longer-line, choppy bob is suitable for medium-textured hair. The hair was styled by rough-drying then working wax through. By Tracie Cant and Ray Wilson for Labothene Academy, Pforzheim, Germany.

Thick hair was taper cut to fall into shape. The hair is slice-coloured with blonde and copper to give this effect. By Schumi, London.

Thick hair was chipped into to give texture. Mousse was worked into the roots and through to the ends then diffuser-dried, lifting hair at the roots to get lift. By Tracie Cant and Ray Wilson for Labothene Academy, Pforzheim, Germany.

Internal layering gives medium-textured hair more body and makes it easier to style. The hair was blow-dried with mousse using a styling brush and a little cream worked through to give texture. By Tracie Cant and Ray Wilson for Labothene Academy, Pforzheim, Germany.

A curved fringe (bangs) adds interest to this short, glossy bob. The hair was styled using a vent brush pointing the barrel of the hairdryer downwards to get a high gloss, and finished with a few drops of serum. By Formulaa Art Team, Formulaa, Norwich, England.

Hair was backcombed then chopped before ruffle-drying with wax. By Antoinette Beenders, The Aveda Concept Salon, Harvey Nichols, London.

Short hair was cut long on the crown and cropped close at the sides. The hair was blow-dried using gel and a vent brush to form hair into a quiff (tuft). By Antoinette Beenders. The Aveda Concept Salon at Harvey Nichols, London.

Above left to right: Variations on short, choppy looks, where the hair is finger-dried with lots of wet-look gel to give an uneven, tousled texture. By Burlingtons Artistic Team, London, for Wella. Photography James Cant.

Fine hair was bleached and cut very short and spiky. The hair was styled using gel spray and dried whilst lifting hair up from scalp. By Pat Dixon, Classics Hair & Beauty, Kenilworth, England. Photography Simon Donnelly.

Above and right: The side hair was blow-dried smooth and the top curled using a round bristle brush to give this bob a different look. By Formulaa Art Team, Formulaa, Norwich, England.

Left: Thick hair was heavily highlighted to break up the texture. The hair was ruffle-dried with mousse using fingers to lift hair from scalp. *Right:* For an alternative look, blow-dry smoother using a vent brush. By Anthony John, Newport, Gwent, Wales. Photography Sanders Nicolson.

Razor cutting thick hair gives a ruffled texture. The hair was blow-dried with mousse, with the hairdryer on high heat and speed setting, and finished with wax. By Pat Wood, Saks Art Team, Durham, England. Photography Chris Lane.

A bob was graduated with point cutting and texturizing of the ends. A fringe (bangs) was cut on to the forehead and textured at the sides. The hair was blow-dried with styling cream. By Tracey Gallagher, Saks Art Team, Durham, England. Photography Chris Lane.

Natural curls were enhanced by clever cutting. The hair was styled using wet-look gel and diffuser-dried to maximize movement. By Gaylord Howlett for Schwarzkopf.

Shades of blonde were used to create this colour effect. The hair was blow-dried using styling lotion and a bristle brush. By Cameron, Cameron H. Hairdressing, Halebarns, Altrincham, England, for Wella. Photography Paul Jones.

Left: A short crop was given interest with a permanent colour in warm burgundy-red. The hair was blow-dried using gel and a round bristle brush. By Ian and Terence, Suyo Hairdressing, Harborne, Birmingham, England, for Wella. Photography Paul Jones.

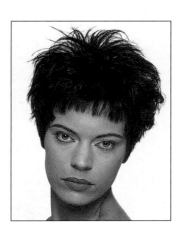

Above: Straight hair was layered all through with longer lengths on the crown. The hair was blast-dried using maximum heat and speed settings and finished by working wax through the ends to create texture. By Sarah Menzies, Keith Hall, the Hairdressers, Leicester, England, for Wella. Photography Alistair Hughes.

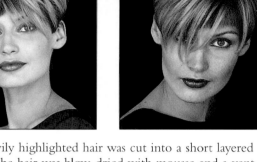

Fine hair was cut to feather on to the face then blow-dried forward from the crown using a little mousse and a styling brush. By John Jenkins, Chobham, Surrey, England, for L'Oréal Professionnel.

Copper lights are worked through the hair from the roots to the ends, then blow-dried forward using a styling brush. By the Hair Business.

Above: Heavily highlighted hair was cut into a short layered crop. *Left:* The hair was blow-dried with mousse and a vent brush for height. *Right:* For a smoother finish, a paddle brush was used. By Andrew Collinge, Liverpool and Harrods, London, for Denman. Photography Trevor Leighton.

A one-length short crop was blow-dried straight, then texture created by using crimping irons on sections of hair. By Charlie Taylor, Charlie Taylor Hair & Beauty, Perth, Scotland. Photography Trevor Leighton.

A short, razored crop is suitable for medium and thick hair. The hair was speed-dried with just a little mousse and finished with a defining wax. By Charlie Taylor, Charlie Taylor Hair & Beauty, Perth, Scotland. Photography Trevor Leighton.

A smooth, cap-like bob was blow-dried flat using a classic styling brush and pointing the nozzle of the hairdryer downwards to encourage cuticles to lie flat and give maximum shine. By Charlie Taylor, Charlie Taylor Hair & Beauty, Perth, Scotland. Photography Trevor Leighton.

STYLE GALLERY, MID-LENGTH HAIR

Hair of medium length can be worn in a sleek bob or lightly layered to give versatility.

Layering gives this 70s-inspired style a fresh look. The hair was misted with styling spray and rough-dried before finishing with a little gloss. By Trevor Sorbie, London. Photography Mark Havrilliak.

Above: Fine, mid-length hair can be made to look thicker by blunt cutting just below ear level. This style can be roller-set and brushed through with a bristle brush to smooth, or simply blow-dried with a round brush. For L'Oréal.

Medium-textured hair was cut into a one-length bob. Styling spray was applied to partially dried hair, which was then wound on large rollers and heat set. After the rollers were removed the hair was brushed into shape. By Charles Worthington, Worthingtons, London, for L'Oréal Coiffure.

A longer, one-length, graduated bob is perfect for thick, straight hair. Add extra shine by using a longer-lasting, semi-permanent colour. By Umberto Giannino, Kidderminster, England, for L'Oréal Coiffure.

A mid-length, bleached bob was scrunch-dried with mousse to give a tousled look. Use a diffuser to encourage more volume. By Stuart Kirby, Eaton Hair Group, Portsmouth, for L'Oréal Coiffure.

A layered cut was permed to give lots of movement. The hair was scrunch-dried, with the head held forward to give maximum volume. By Anthony Mascalo, Tony & Guy, London, for L'Oréal Coiffure.

A bob was highlighted using a light, golden-blonde colour to give natural, warm lights, then styled and blow-dried using a soft sculpting spray. By Barbara Daley Hair Studio, Liverpool, England, for L'Oréal Coiffure.

A razor-cut bob gives graduation so the hair moves freely. The hair was coloured with a shade of mahogany to give more depth, and then blow-dried using mousse. For L'Oréal.

Left: Thick hair was cut into a bob, then sprayed with styling lotion before setting on large rollers. After drying, the hair was brushed through to give a smooth style that is full of volume. *Right:* The same cut was blow-dried smooth using a styling brush. By Mond Hair, France, for Schwarzkopf.

A smooth, graduated bob was cut long at the sides and shorter into the back. To add additional tone and shine use a longer-lasting, semi-permanent colour, which also gives gloss. Blow-dry straight using a styling brush to smooth the ends under. For L'Oréal.

Left: Natural movement was encouraged by blunt cutting and leaving the hair to dry naturally. Alternatively, the hair could be dried using a flat diffuser attachment on the dryer. *Right:* The same style was sprayed with styling lotion and set on large rollers. When the rollers were removed the hair was ruffled through with the fingers, not brushed. By Regis, Europe. Photography John Swannell.

Thick, straight hair was heavily highlighted and cut into a blunt, short bob. Either blow-dry or leave to dry naturally. By Yosh Toya, San Francisco. Photography Gen.

Left: Wavy hair was cut in short layers. Layers encourage more curl and movement and give a soft, feminine style. The hair was dried using mousse and lifted with the fingers while drying to get height on the crown. By Cobella, London, for Schwarzkopf. Photography Martin Evening.

Left: A soft body perm gives volume to this one-length bob. The hair was gently dried using mousse for additional lift. By Yosh Toya, San Francisco. Photography Gen.

The hair was layered in slices to give movement. Blow-dry using mousse and a styling brush to create texture, flicking the hair out as it dries. By Lara Johnson, Mumbles, Swansea, Wales. Photography David Fernandez.

A long-line bob was blow-dried smooth with gel, then the crown hair was backcombed lightly and smoothed over and finished with a few drops of serum lightly glossed over the surface of the hair. By Lara Johnson, Mumbles, Swansea, Wales, Photography David Fernandez.

To achieve a more ruffled flick-up, dry hair with a styling brush then use a small round bristle brush to create more movement on small sections at a time. By Lara Johnson, Mumbles, Swansea, Wales. Photography David Fernandez.

A simple, long bob can be transformed easily by ...

... a zigzag centre parting ...

... a side parting ...

Left: Natural curls were cut to follow movement, then gel worked all the way through and the hair left to dry naturally. As the hair dries, continue to lift from the head to encourage curl formation. By Labothene Academy, Pforzheim, Germany.

Smooth and sleek, this long-line bob was enhanced with deep copper permanent colour and then misted with spray shine. By Edward Hemmings, Alan d, London, for Schwarzkopf.

... clipping hair across the forehead ...

... a messy parting combined with using straightening irons on sections ...

... and up at the crown into a spiky ponytail. By The Hair Exchange, Milton Keynes, England.

A one-line, point-cut bob is good for fine hair. Blow-dry using styling spray and smooth hair with serum for maximum shine. By Tracie Cant and Ray Wilson for Labothene Academy, Pforzheim, Germany.

An ebony vegetable colour gives the deepest colour. A fine, longer-line bob has chipped in ends, so flick-ups are easy. By Tracie Cant and Ray Wilson for Labothene Academy, Pforzheim, Germany.

The ends of this cut were chipped into to give texture and interest. A few strands of hair were highlighted to break up the front. By Tracie Cant and Ray Wilson for Labothene Academy, Pforzheim, Germany.

A one-length bob was coloured creamy blonde using tint. The hair was blow-dried smooth using a low heat and speed setting and finished with styling cream. By Labothene Academy, Pforzheim, Germany.

Above: Texturizing the ends of the hair gives a new feel to the classic bob. Blow-dry with a large round brush to get a little volume at the roots then tip ends under using a medium sized round brush. *Above right:* For a different look, flick ends out and hold with hairspray. By Sarah Hodge Hairdressing Group, Somerset, England. Photography Sanders Nicolson.

Slices of hair were bleached blonde to give an interesting texture. The hair was rough-dried from the crown using a high heat and speed setting, and wax was worked through the hair to finish. By Tracie Cant and Ray Wilson for Labothene Academy, Pforzheim, Germany.

A jaw-length bob was first towel-dried, then mousse applied for volume. The hair was blow-dried using a large round brush sweeping the front forward. Self-holding rollers were used to give height. By Andrew Collinge, Liverpool and Harrods, London, for Salon Solutions.

A bleached blonde, blunt-cut bob needs regular conditioning and intensive treatments to keep it shiny and beautiful. By Andrew Collinge, Liverpool and Harrods, London, for Salon Solutions.

Black and deep red combine to give this bob a vibrant look. By Andrew Collinge, Liverpool and Harrods, London, for Salon Solutions.

A lightly layered longer-line bob was ruffle-dried using gel and a diffuser attachment on the dryer to get a tousled effect. By Andrew Collinge, Liverpool and Harrods, London, for Salon Solutions.

A longer-length, straight bob can be blow-dried smooth or ruffled, then sections smoothed with flat irons for a different, more modern feel. By Burlingtons, London.

Centre partings look good on one-length cuts. Blow-dry with styling spray to eliminate static, wrapping ends under a large bristle brush to get movement. By Martyn Maxey, Martyn Maxey Hairdressing, London.

A simple bob can be transformed with colour ... an all-over blonde tint ...

... a vegetable shine rinse ...

... or a few blonde lights.
By Yosh Toya, Yosh for Hair,
San Francisco. Photography Gen.

Texture was achieved by using straightening irons on small sections of hair. By Mark Smith, Staffords, The House That Hair Built, Leigh-on-Sea, Essex, England, for Yum Yum. Photography Dean Chalky.

Poker-straight hair was blunt cut to fall free. The hair was blast-dried from the crown using gel and a high speed setting. By John Carne, Guildford, England. Photography Stewart Weston.

A bleached blonde was blunt cut with disconnected layers to give a multi-textured finish. By John Carne, Guildford, England. Photography Stewart Weston.

Chin-length layers balance with longer lengths. The hair was styled by blow-drying using styling spray and a round brush. By John Carne, Guildford, England. Photography Stewart Weston.

The hair was blow-dried straight then the ends tonged to achieve mini-flicks. For Wella Experience. Photography Iain Philpott.

A lightly layered bob was set on rollers, then brushed with a bristle brush to get smoothness. An ideal style for curly hair. By David Richards, John Jenkins, Chobham, Surrey, England, for L'Oréal Professionnel.

Above left: Razor cutting gives this style movement and versatility. The hair was rough-dried using mousse and finished with wax. *Above right:* For a smoother finish, work into shape using styling cream and your fingers. By Sean Hanna, Wimbledon, London.

Left: Softness on this style was achieved by rough-drying, then setting on self-holding rollers and misting with styling spray. The hair was heat set with a diffuser for a few minutes before removing rollers and brushing through. By Sharon Malcolm, Hair Traffic, Belfast, N. Ireland.

Thick, straight hair was blow-dried back from the face to give a lift at the front. By Formulaa Art Team, Formulaa, Norwich, England.

The hair was cut into a jaw-length bob with heavy razor-cut layers. Mousse and wax were applied and straightening irons used from root to tip to give shattered ends. By Tomy, Moga, London. Photography Terence Renati.

Movement was achieved with a light perm that gives body and hold. The hair was roller set for smoothness and finished using a bristle brush. By Keith Harris for Wella. Photography Sanders Nicolson.

A long-line fringe (bangs) combines with a longer bob for this modern look. Leave until nearly dry, add a little smoothing gel and blow-dry gently to get rid of any frizz. Hair by Pat Wood, Saks Art Team, Durham, England.

Point cutting makes hair sit neatly into the neck. The hair was smoothed straight by blow-drying and polished with a few drops of serum warmed between palms before use. By Johanna Cree, The Rainbow Room, Glasgow, for Schwarzkopf.

A choppy cut was blow-dried with a vent brush and flicked out to achieve movement. By Anthony John, Newport, Gwent, Wales. Photography Sanders Nicolson.

Permanent shades of blonde were used to get this effect, then the hair was styled using shine cream before blow-drying. By David Jones, Keith Hall, the Hairdressers for Wella. Photography Alistair Hughes.

Heavy-duty wax redefines a classic long bob into a modern look. By Cutting Club, Cleethorpes, Lincolnshire, England. Photography Chris Bishop.

Straight hair was given a new look with blonde streaks and, after blow-drying, strands were allowed to fall over the fringe. By Sarah Hodge Hairdressing, Somerset and Devon, England. Photography Sanders Nicolson.

A simple bob can be ...
... blow-dried forward ...

... tucked behind the ear ...

... or ruffled.
By Ellen Colin and Taylor Ferguson, Taylor Ferguson, Glasgow, Scotland. Photography Taylor Ferguson.

Hair with slight natural movement can be ... blow-dried smooth ...

... ruffle-dried with a diffuser ...

... or gelled and left natural. By Ellen Colin and Taylor Ferguson, Taylor Ferguson, Glasgow, Scotland. Photography Taylor Ferguson.

The fringe was smoothed over and the ends flicked out, to give this a modernist edge. By Anthony John, Newport, Gwent, Wales. Photography Sanders Nicolson.

Texture was achieved by combining root tonging with backcombing for this fresh, funky look. By Formulaa Art Team, Formulaa, Norwich, England.

The ends of fine hair were clipped into, so it can be dressed out or under. By Anthony John, Newport, Gwent, Wales. Photography Sanders Nicolson.

After drying, wax was worked through the hair to give separation and texture. By Anthony John, Newport, Gwent, Wales. Photography Sanders Nicolson.

Lightly layered hair was set on self-holding rollers when nearly dry, then diffuser-set. The rollers were removed and the hair lightly backcombed, misted with hairspray and arranged with fingers. By Anthony John, Newport, Gwent, Wales. Photography Sanders Nicolson.

Thick hair was blow-dried to even out the texture, then ruffled with wax. By Anthony John, Newport, Gwent, Wales. Photography Sanders Nicolson.

Natural curls were diffuser-dried with gel and the head held upside-down to give maximum lift. By Anthony John, Newport, Gwent, Wales. Photography Sanders Nicolson.

Rough-drying a classic bob using the dryer on high heat and speed gives a ruffled finish. By Anthony John. Newport, Gwent, Wales. Photography Sanders Nicolson.

Rough-dried hair was misted with hairspray then blasted again with the dryer for lots of volume and movement. By Anthony John, Newport, Gwent, Wales. Photography Sanders Nicolson.

A smooth, one-length bob was gelled and blow-dried flat using a styling brush. By Anthony John, Newport, Gwent, Wales. Photography Sanders Nicolson.

Thick hair was cut to flick out, then styled using mousse and a round bristle brush, encouraging hair to curve up and out. By Joseph and Jane Harling, Avon, England.

Hair was rough-dried then straightening irons were used to get spiky separation. By Antoinette Beenders, The Aveda Concept Salon, Harvey Nichols, London.

Above left and right: Layer cuts can be blow-dried so they look wild and free or smoothed straighter and flatter to the head for daytime wear. By Andrew Collinge, Liverpool and Harrods London, for Denman. Photography Trevor Leighton.

Slightly wavy hair was cut to tame movement. The hair was blow-dried using a classic styling brush and finished with a few drops of serum to eliminate frizz. By Labothene Academy, Pforzheim, Germany.

A soft, longer-line fringe (bangs) sets off this longer-length bob which can be left to dry naturally, then the ends tonged to achieve flick-ups. By Joseph and Jane Harling, Avon, England. Photography Barry Cook.

One-length hair looks good worn behind the ears with the ends flicked out. By Tina Shaw, Dimensions Hair Salon, Sheffield, England.

A layered cut was blow-dried with strong gel, then backcombed at roots for volume. By Joseph and Jane Harling, Avon, England. Photography Iain Philpott.

A one-length cut was rough-dried then set on heated rollers. Rollers were left to cool before removing, then hair raked through using fingers, to keep maximum amount of curl. By Joseph and Jane Harling, Avon. Photography Barry Cook.

A one-length bob can be worn in many ways ... smooth from a side parting on the right ...

... or on the left ...

... or the hair can be blow-dried forward ...

... or slicked from the crown. By Kaye Volante and Rebecca Maher, Gregory Couzens, Rochdale, England for Wella. Photography Alistair Hughes.

The hair was blow-dried smooth straight back from the hairline and ends flicked out using a round bristle brush. By John Jenkins, Chobham and Sunningdale, England for L'Oréal Professionnel.

Flick-ups can be ... glamorous for evening wear ...

... or sophisticated for daytime.
By John Jenkins, Chobham and Sunningdale, England for L'Oréal Professionnel. Photography David Richards.

A tint in copper gives vibrant colour to this longer-line choppy cut which was blow-dried forward and misted with shine spray for extra gloss. By Sarah Lucas, Keith Hall, the Hairdressers, Leicester, England, for Wella.

STYLE GALLERY, LONG HAIR

Long hair can be waved, curled,
or left to fall free.

Naturally wavy hair was roller-set and heat-dried before brushing through lightly. A similar look could be achieved with a soft perm. By Steven Carey, London.

After an application of styling spray, the hair was set on large rollers. When dry, the hair was combed to one side and allowed to fall into soft waves, with a tiny tendril pulled in front of one ear. By Neville Daniel, London, for Lamaur.

Long, straight hair was graduated at the sides to give interest. It was then shampooed and conditioned, and left to dry naturally. By Neville Daniel, London, for Lamaur.

A vegetable colour adds depth and makes hair appear even thicker. The hair was then simply styled by blow-drying. By Daniel Galvin, London.

Soft, undulating waves were achieved by tonging the hair, then lightly combing it through. Spray shine was applied to the finish. By Nicky Clarke, London.

Thick hair was cut with graduated sides and a heavy fringe (bangs) to give this 60s look. The hair can be blow-dried smooth or left to dry naturally. By John Frieda, London and New York.

Setting lotion was applied to clean hair, which was set on large rollers and heat dried. When the hair was completely dry, the rollers were removed and the hair gently back-combed at the roots to give even more height and fullness. By Daniel Galvin, London.

Far left: The hair was shampooed and conditioned, then rough-dried before applying mousse and setting on heated rollers. The hair was then brushed through into soft waves. *Left:* This alternative style was achieved by tonging. It could also be set on shapers. For Silvikrin, London.

Left: A thick, graduated cut was given maximum lift by spraying the roots with gel spray and backcombing lightly, then brushing over the top layers. By Daniel Galvin, London.

Naturally wavy hair was lightly layered, then set on large rollers. When the hair was dry it was brushed lightly to give broken-up waves and curls. By Daniel Galvin, London.

The hair was sprayed with styling lotion and set on heated rollers. When it was dry, a bristle brush was used to smooth it into waves. By Adam Lyons, Grays, Essex, England, for L'Oreal Coiffure.

Above: Coarse hair was rough dried and then tonged all over before brushing through to give a soft movement. By Keith Harris for Braun.

Left: Long, straight hair was blunt-cut at the ends and simply styled from a centre parting. By Taylor Ferguson, Glasgow, Scotland.

Left: To give one-length hair extra body, the head was tipped forwards and the hair misted with sculpting lotion. The roots were scrunched a little with the hands before straightening the head. By Paul Falltrick, Falltricks, Essex, England, for Clynol. Photography Alistair Hughes.

TAKE ONE GIRL

The following styles illustrate how one-length hair can be transformed using different styling techniques.

1 Soft waves were created with rollers.

2 The top hair was clipped up and the back hair tonged into tendrils.

3 High bunches were carefully secured and the hair crimped.

4 The top hair was secured on the crown. A band was wrapped with a small piece of hair and the length allowed to fall freely.

5 The hair was clipped back and two simple braids were worked at each side.

Hair by Taylor Ferguson, Glasgow, Scotland.

Layers give movement to long hair. Blow-dry, then use a large barrel tong to curve ends out. Use a bristle brush for daily grooming as it will keep long hair shiny. By Sean Hanna and Sean Dawson, Sean Hanna, Wimbledon, London for L'Oréal Professionnel.

Very long black hair was given a new look with streaks of bright red running through the fringe. The hair was left to dry naturally with a little wax worked through to give separation. By Antoinette Beenders, The Aveda Concept Salon, Harvey Nichols, London.

Hair was coloured using henna which brings out natural red tones. The result of henna application is permanent and, although it fades, it stays in the hair until it is cut, so always do a test strand if you want to use a chemical colour after using henna. By Jonathan Woodward, Greta Kahn, London & Austria.

A longer-lasting semi-permanent was used to give this brilliant copper colour. By Harry Boocock and Chris Horsman, The Hair Studio for Schwarzkopf.

Waves were achieved on long hair by blow-drying then tonging. A few drops of serum applied to outer layers banish frizz. By Martyn Maxey, Martyn Maxey Hairdressing, London.

Long hair that has been lightened more than a couple of shades should be left to dry naturally and finished with a little wax to combat static. By Joseph and Jane Harling, Avon, England.

A different texture is achieved by tonging sections and leaving roots and ends straight. After tonging, simply rake through with fingers. By Antoinette Beenders, The Aveda Concept Salon, Harvey Nichols, London.

Straight hair was tapered at the sides to lie flat to the head but with a little flick at the shoulder line. Hair was blow-dried smooth with a bristle brush. By Tracie Cant and Ray Wilson, Labothene Academy, Pforzheim, Germany.

A growing-out fringe can be swept across the forehead and tucked behind one ear. Here, brilliant red permanent colour gives a vibrant style. By Tracie Cant and Ray Wilson, Labothene Academy, Pforzheim, Germany.

A long-line bob was lightly layered at the ends so it can be rough-dried to give texture. A vibrant copper semi-permanent was used to give a stunning colour. By Andrew Collinge, Liverpool and Harrods, London, for Salon Solutions.

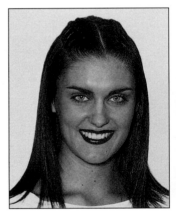

Straight hair is coloured with a red-violet permanent tint. Hair was blow-dried straight, then two sections, either side of a centre parting, plaited and secured at the crown. Hair by David Adams, The Urban Retreat and Aveda Concept Salon, Harvey Nichols, London. Photography Alistair Hughes.

Two-tone colouring works well on straight hair. Here, streaks of copper blend through brown to give a different colour result. By David Adams, The Aveda Concept Salon, Harvey Nichols, London.

A slightly graduated, shoulder-length bob was blow-dried using mousse and a paddle brush which has widely spaced teeth that won't drag the hair. By Wella Experience. Photography Iain Philpott.

Strip lights – a bolder version of highlights – give this graduated cut wide streaks of colour. Rough dry, apply styling spray, and set on heated or self-holding rollers to give movement and just a little bounce and curl. By Martyn Maxey, Martyn Maxey Hairdressing, London.

Heavy graduation at the sides gives this long style lots of bounce. The hair was blow-dried using mousse and a large round bristle brush, working on one section of hair at a time and flicking the ends out. By Martyn Maxey, Martyn Maxey Hairdressing, London.

To obtain movement on straight hair, it was first rough-dried then set on heated rollers. Leave rollers to cool completely before removing and then use a brush with widely spaced teeth to gently loosen curl. By Sharon Malcolm, Hair Traffic, Belfast, N. Ireland.

Smooth, long-line bobs should be dried using mousse and a large paddle brush. Dry one section of hair at a time, making sure it is completely dry before moving to the next. By Sharon Malcolm, Hair Traffic, Belfast, N. Ireland.

A bleached-blonde, layered cut was blast-dried with mousse, ruffling with hands to give texture. The hair was finished by running a little wax through mid-lengths to the ends. By Nick Wilding, La Vie en Rose, Cheshunt, Herts, England. Photography Mauro Cararro.

Thick hair was graduated and the sides then blow-dried straight using a styling spray. The hair was coloured chestnut with a semi-permanent. By Nick Wilding, La Vie en Rose, Cheshunt, Herts, England.

Long layers were given a new look by scooping the crown hair up into a ponytail and allowing lengths to fall. Finish with shine spray. By Terry Calvert, Clipso, Watford, Hemel Hempstead and St. Albans, England.

The ends were chipped into to give texture. The hair was styled with gel, combed into shape then left to dry naturally. By Terry Calvert, Clipso, Watford, Hemel Hempstead and St. Albans, England. Photography Martin Evening.

A zigzag parting, which is easy to do with the end of a tail-comb, gives a one-length, long cut a fresh new slant. By Edward Hemmings, Alan d, London.

A choppy, disconnected cut is easy to style: just apply gel and comb in place. By Barbara Daley, Liverpool, England for L'Oréal Professionnel.

Disconnected layers look great on black hair. The hair was styled using gel. By Barbara Daley, Liverpool, England for L'Oréal Professionnel.

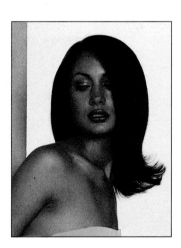

Long flick-ups were achieved by first blow-drying hair straight, then using a large barrel tong to flick the ends out. By Michael Aronberg, W1 Hair Design, Ilford, Essex, England. Photography Chris Bishop.

A choppy cut gives lift to heavy hair. The hair was blow-dried with mousse, using a round bristle brush to get width at the sides, and finished by working wax through. By Robert Bell, Woodford Green, Essex, England.

For a different look, long hair was partially tonged in small sections then gel applied and texture achieved with fingers. By Giovanni Ieronimo at Cutting Club, Cleethorpes, Lincolnshire, England. Photography Chris Bishop.

Graduated blonding, where shades of lightness run through the hair, gives a lovely look to one-length hair. By Antoinette Beenders, The Aveda Concept Salon, Harvey Nichols, London.

Long layers give movement to thick hair which is blow-dried with mousse. By Labothene Academy, Pforzheim, Germany.

Graduation on long hair means it can be dried straight, but the effect is tousled and a little unkempt. Texture through the lengths is achieved with wax. By Saks Art Team, Co. Durham, England.

The hair was lightly layered to give lift and the ends coloured slightly darker. Blow-dried with mousse to get fullness and smoothness. By Taryn MacGregor, London. Photography John Rowley.

Shorter layers at the sides and chipped-in ends. Blow-dry with mousse for volume and get separation by working wax through ends. By Nicole Rees, Lifestyle, Hull, England for Wella. Photography Alistair Hughes.

Thick hair is rough-dried, then set on self-holding rollers and misted with hairspray. Heat set for a few minutes, allow hair to cool, then brush through. By Joseph and Jane Harling, Avon, England. Photography Barry Cook.

A few blonde streaks around the front break up the heaviness of thick hair. Leave to dry naturally. By Goldsworthy's for L'Oréal Professionnel.

Dead-straight hair was boldly streaked with blonde and blow-dried smooth using a little mousse and a paddle brush. By Andrew Collinge, Liverpool and Harrods, London, for Denman. Photography Trevor Leighton.

Copper lowlights add interest to the front, as long hair is swept back and shorter layers left to fall freely around the face. By John Carne for L'Oréal Professionnel.

Internal layering gives a shaggy finish to this long-line bob. The hair was blow-dried with liquid gel to achieve gloss and smoothness. By Tracie Cant and Ray Wilson, Labothene Academy, Pforzheim, Germany.

The hair was coloured deep black with a permanent tint and blow-dried straight. For a different look, the top hair was scooped up and secured at centre back. By Sean Hanna for L'Oréal Professionnel.

Lowlights were worked through the crown of this layered, long-line bob. The hair was rough-dried with mousse, then ends were tonged, to achieve flick-ups. By Level One for L'Oréal Professionnel.

STYLE GALLERY, SPECIAL OCCASIONS

These styles will inspire you when you want to dress up mid-length or long hair on those special occasions.

The hair was softly scooped into large curls and pinned in place. One tendril was left to fall free to soften the style. By Zotos International.

The foundation for this style came from a roller-set. The back hair was then formed into a French pleat (roll) and the top hair looped, curled and pinned in place. The side tendrils were allowed to fall free. Hair by Regis, Europe. Photography Mark York.

Very curly hair was simply twisted up at the back and secured with pins. Curls were allowed to fall down on one side to give a feminine look. By Steven Carey, London. Photography Alistair Hughes.

The hair was secured in a very high ponytail on the crown, then divided into sections and looped into curls. If your hair isn't long enough for this style, you could use a hairpiece. By Steven Carey, London. Photography Alistair Hughes.

Long hair was scooped up, but the essence of this style is to allow lots of strands to fall in soft curls around the face. By Partners, London.

Vibrant blonde and copper lights add brilliance to the hair. The front hair was sectioned off and the back hair secured in a high ponytail. The hair was then divided and coiled into loops before pinning in place. The front hair was smoothed over and secured at the back. For Schwarzkopf.

A high ponytail forms the basis of this style. The hair was then looped into curls and pinned, and the fringe (bangs) was combed to one side. Hair by Keith Harris for Braun.

Slice colour in tones of red and blonde give brilliant colour. The roots were backcombed vigorously and the hair misted with strong-hold hairspray, making sure it was applied to the root area. By Lara Johnson, Mumbles, Swansea, Wales. Photography David Fernandez.

The hair was scooped into a high ponytail on the crown, twisted round and secured. The ends were left to splay out. A long fringe (bangs) was divided, defined with wet-look gel and combed into strands. By Edward Hemmings, Alan d, London, for Schwarzkopf.

The crown hair was twisted into a topknot and tied on top of the head. The ends were allowed to fall free with a strand pulled down from the ponytail and left loose. By Anthony John, Newport, Gwent, Wales. Photography Sanders Nicolson.

Transform short hair for the evening by backcombing heavily at the roots and applying strong-hold gel spray. Side hair can be slicked back. By Nicky Oliver, Manchester, England, for Schwarzkopf. Photography Alan Pickering.

Clip hair up into a loose knot on the crown, allowing the ends to splay out. Pull pieces of hair down over the fringe (bangs), working gel through each strand to give separation. By Martin Cox, Sutton Coldfield, England. Photography Martin Cox.

Or smooth the hair up into a pleat (roll), leaving the ends to splay out as before and pulling strands of hair down, working gel through to separate. By Martin Cox, Sutton Coldfield, England. Photography Martin Cox.

First, set dry hair on heated rollers to give curl, then scoop into a ponytail at back and allow the crown hair to pile on top of the head. Backcomb as necessary to get height and mist with hairspray to hold. By Martine Finnegan, Natural Hair Company, Lisburn, N. Ireland. Photography Rick Bond.

Afro-style hair was clasped in a high ponytail and the ends left to fan out. Wax was worked through the hair to give curl separation and extra texture. By Formulaa Art Team, Formulaa, Norwich, England.

The crown hair was backcombed, smoothed and clipped at the centre back. By Nicky Oliver, Manchester, England, for Schwarzkopf. Photography Alan Pickering.

The hair was smoothed from one side into a pleat (roll) at the back and the ends allowed to form a tuft, then pinned in place with a section of side hair allowed to fall in front of the ear. By Martine Finnegan, Natural Hair Company, Lisburn, N. Ireland. Photography Rick Bond.

The hair was slicked back with gel to a ponytail on one side of the head. The ponytail was twisted round once, then the ends divided into two and backcombed to form fans. The hair was pinned up and held with hairspray. By Giovanni Ieronimo, Cutting Club, Cleethorpes, Lincolnshire, England. Photography Chris Bishop.

Mid-length, straight hair was given an evening look by taking small sections of hair and twisting and gripping into place. By Tracie Cant and Ray Wilson for Labothene Academy, Pforzheim, Germany.

A classic chignon, where sections of hair were smoothed over and criss-crossed. The back hair was twisted into a neat pleat (roll). By Richard Ward, Richard Ward Hair & Beauty, London.

Sections of mid-length hair were knotted and the ends left to fall free. Gel was worked through the hair to give gloss. By Charlie Taylor, Charlie Taylor Hair & Beauty, Perth, Scotland. Photography Trevor Leighton.

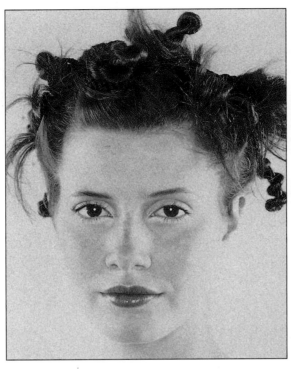

The hair was divided into sections and each one twisted until it rolled back on itself, then pinned in place. Repeat all over the head. By Charlie Taylor, Charlie Taylor Hair & Beauty, Perth, Scotland. Photography Trevor Leighton.

Mid-length hair was randomly backcombed, then pinned up to create an unstructured, casual upstyle. By Charlie Taylor, Charlie Taylor Hair & Beauty, Perth, Scotland. Photography Trevor Leighton.

Thick, lightly-layered hair was scooped up into a ponytail on the crown and the ends allowed to fan out. The hair was misted with hairspray to hold it in place. By Silvikrin.

Mid-length hair can be dressed up by applying gel and taking one small section at a time, twisting the hair and pinning in place. Repeat all over the head. By Giovanni Ieronimo, Cutting Club, Cleethorpes, Lincolnshire, England. Photography Chris Bishop.

One-length, long hair was twisted into a coil at the nape of the neck and pinned in place. The side and some back hair was left to hang loose. By Anthony John, Newport, Gwent, Wales. Photography Sanders Nicolson.

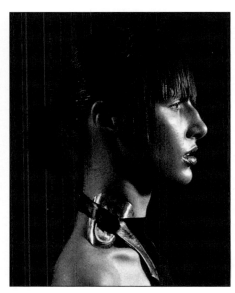

A classic chignon where the hair was smoothed and rolled round a pad, the ends were then tucked in and pinned. Lengths of fringe hair (bangs) were left to fall. By Martyn Maxey, Martyn Maxey Hairdressing, London.

For an evening out hair can be quickly and temporarily coloured using a semi-permanent shampoo-in product. By Wella Shaders and Toners.

A modern-style ponytail was scraped back with gel and a section of hair twisted round to disguise the hairband. The fringe (bangs) and side hair was combed straight. By John Carne Artistic Team, Guildford, Surrey, England.

Top knots

Variations on the top knot ...
... hair is scooped into a high ponytail and a band of hair wound round to cover the band, then ends backcombed to fan out ...

... tiny sections of hair are twisted and pinned – this is suitable for quite short hair ...

... back hair is pleated (rolled) into a chignon and the ends backcombed with the fringe (bangs) slicked neatly forward. By Andrew Collinge, Liverpool and Harrods, London for Salon Solutions.

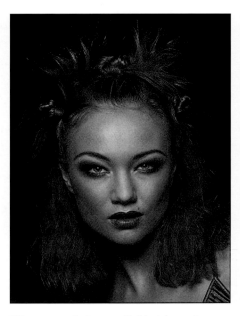

Sections of hair were twisted and pinned into place, then the ends backcombed to fan out. The hair was misted with strong-hold hairspray to keep the look. By Sharon Malcolm, Hair Traffic, Belfast, N. Ireland.

The crown hair was divided into three pieces which were twisted and pinned into place. The lower hair was crimped. By Sharon Malcolm, Hair Traffic, Belfast, N.Ireland.

The hair was coloured using colour gel applied with fingers to damp hair. A combination of blue and gold was used here and the hair clipped up. By Wella Shockwaves.

Thick hair was twisted up into a high chignon and the ends formed into large curls. The look was softened by allowing a tendril of hair to fall over the face. By Elizabeth Lambert, Mark Hill, Hull, England. Photography Alan Burton.

The hair was pinned into a ponytail at the nape of the neck, then briskly backcombed and sprayed with strong-hold gel before fanning out. By Joanna Cree, The Rainbow Room, Glasgow, Scotland for Schwarzkopf.

The crown hair was sectioned off and backcombed at the roots, then smoothed back and pinned. Sections were then looped into curls and pinned. By Derek Preston, Klownz, Edinburgh, Scotland.

Highlighted hair was backcombed lightly at the roots and clasped up into a high ponytail. The hair was pinned at random and backcombed for texture. The fringe hair (bangs) was combed straight. By Nicole Rees, Lifestyle, Hull for Wella. Photography Alistair Hughes.

Hair was blow-dried smooth, then brushed into a high ponytail. The hair was wound round and held with strong-hold gel. By Martine Finnegan, Natural Hair Company, Lisburn, N. Ireland.

A long, layered cut is set off by a curved fringe (bangs). A small section of hair on the crown was clipped up into a small ponytail and the ends backcombed. By Lara Johnson, Mumbles, Swansea, Wales.

The hair was gelled then sections tied into loose knots. A section of hair on the crown was twisted into soft spikes. By Giovanni Ieronimo, Cutting Club, Cleethorpes, Lincolnshire, England.

Naturally curly hair was diffuser-dried for maximum curl and twisted at the back and secured. The top hair was separated out using fingers. By Studio One, Edinburgh, Scotland.

Long, naturally wavy hair was sectioned off at the front, which was smoothed flat. The back hair was pinned up at random and sections allowed to fall into waves. By Ian Robertson, Ian Robertson International, Kilmarnock, Scotland.

The hair was crimped all over then misted with gel spray, especially on the roots. A zigzag hair-band was then pushed into place. By Joseph and Jane Harling, Avon, England. Photography Barry Cook.

Mid-length hair was clipped up a section at a time, then twisted and pinned into place. The ends were coated with gel and the hair formed into spikes. By Studio One, Edinburgh, Scotland.

Mid-length, fine hair was pinned up in random sections which were then lightly backcombed and misted with hairspray. By Joseph and Jane Harling, Avon, England. Photography Barry Cook.

The hair was scooped into a high ponytail and the ends fanned using a vent brush. The style held with a fine mist of hairspray. By Andrew Collinge, Liverpool and Harrods, London, for Denman. Photography Trevor Leighton.

The hair was twisted into looped curls and pinned into place. A feathered head-dress completes the 'pretty as a picture' look. By Andrew Collinge, Liverpool and Harrods, London, for Salon Solutions.

Long hair was blow-dried smooth then crimped all over. The crown hair was pinned up and formed into spikes. By Joseph and Jane Harling, Avon, England. Photography Barry Cook.

For an alternative look, the hair was swept up at the back. By Joseph and Jane Harling, Avon, England. Photography Barry Cook.

The hair was parted on the side and lightly backcombed, then pinned up in sections on to the crown. By Joseph and Jane Harling, Avon, England. Photography Barry Cook.

Straight, layered hair was divided into sections and twisted back on itself. Each section was secured with pins. This was repeated all over. By Joseph and Jane Harling, Avon, England. Photography Barry Cook.

Naturally curly hair was diffuser-dried with mousse to give curl separation and volume. The hair was clipped up on the crown and held with hairspray. By Joseph and Jane Harling, Avon, England. Photography Barry Cook.

The hair was pinned up in a circle of grips (pins) round the crown, then small sections taken and each backcombed and rolled into a curl before pinning into place. By Tina Shaw, Dimensions Sheffield, England for Goldwell.

A parting was made on one side of the head to the other and the hair twisted and knotted, then secured with pins. This was repeated over the crown until all the hair was dressed. By Joseph and Jane Harling, Avon, England. Photography Barry Cook.

The top hair was sectioned off and divided into five sections which were tied into knots with the ends kicking out. The lower hair was braided and bound with ribbon. By Joseph and Jane Harling, Avon, England. Photography Barry Cook.

Heated rollers were used to give the hair a foundation set. When the rollers were cool they were removed and the hair was backcombed, misted with gel spray before smoothing the front and fanning out the back. By Joseph and Jane Harling, Avon, England. Photography Barry Cook.

STYLE GALLERY, CURLY HAIR

Natural, permed or tonged curls can be worn in many different ways.

Natural corkscrew curls were coated with leave-in conditioner and left to dry. By Michael Aronberg, W1 Hair Design, Ilford, Essex, England. Photography Chris Bishop.

The hair was permed using a twisting technique which gives lots of texture. Hair is diffuser-dried with gel spray and the head held upside-down, with definition created using wax. By L'Oréal Professionnel.

A volumizing perm gives bounce to mid-length layers. The hair was rough-dried, then set on self-holding rollers and heat set. When the hair was quite cool, the rollers were removed and the hair raked through to give a tousled finish. By Martine Finnegan, Natural Hair Company, Lisburn, N. Ireland.

Curls were piled round a cone base – available from hairdressing salons – and pinned into place. By Formulaa Art Team, Formulaa, Norwich, England.

Curls were diffuser-dried, then tiny sections were braided at random to give different textures. By Formulaa Art Team, Formulaa, Norwich, England.

This is another variation on the twist perm which gives masses of movement and bounce. By L'Oréal Professionnel.

Corkscrew curls were eased out a little using a wide-toothed Afro comb. By Charlie Taylor, Charlie Taylor Hair & Beauty, Perth, Scotland. Photography Trevor Leighton.

The hair was tonged using tongs with a small barrel to smooth natural curl and give bounce to each tendril. By Sean Hanna, Wimbledon, London.

Permed, layered hair was set on self-holding rollers to smooth curl and give control. By Sharon Malcolm, Hair Traffic, Belfast, N.Ireland.

Naturally very curly hair was straightened by blow-drying, then scooped up and the curls tonged for definition. By Sharon Malcolm, Hair Traffic, Belfast, N.Ireland.

Straight-haired girls can create curls by tonging hair in small sections. By Sharon Malcolm, Hair Traffic, Belfast, N.Ireland.

Natural curls were diffuser-dried using gel spray. Curl formation can be re-activated the next day by misting hair with water. For an alternative look, curls are gently teased out using an Afro comb. By Staffords, The House That Hair Built, Leigh-on-Sea, Essex, England. Photography Mark Smith.

Short hair was cut in layers to follow curl formation, then styled by applying mousse and diffuser-drying before working a little wax through the hair to give separation. By Sharon Malcolm, Hair Traffic, Belfast, N. Ireland.

Permed, lightly-layered hair was partially dried then set on medium-sized rollers and heat set. When the hair was cool, the rollers were removed and the head tilted forward and the hair misted with gel spray. By Martyn Maxey, Martyn Maxey Hairdressing, London. Photography Maura Cararro.

A texturizing perm gives volume and curls. The hair was diffuser-dried with mousse and finished with a little wax to give hair definition. By Yosh for Hair, San Francisco. Photography Gen.

Natural curls were pinned back at the sides, and the top hair diffuser-dried to give volume. Wax was worked through the ends of the hair to give separation. By Lara Johnson, Mumbles, Swansea, Wales. Photography David Fernandez.

Natural curls were given even more texture by tonging random sections throughout the hair. By John Carne Artistic Team, Guildford, Surrey, England.

Natural curls were highlighted to give definition. The hair was then diffuser-dried. By Joseph and Jane Harling, Avon, England. Photography Barry Cook.

Straight, one-length hair was tonged to give these beautiful curls. By Joseph and Jane Harling, Avon, England. Photography Barry Cook.

Tight, natural curls were clasped to the crown with a zigzag hair-band which was fixed at the nape. By Terry Calvert, Clipso, Watford, Hemel Hempstead and St. Albans, England. Photography Martin Evening.

Slightly wavy hair was set on small rollers to give lots of curl. When the hair was dry, the front hair was smoothed with a bristle brush whilst the back hair was formed into curls. By Pat Dixon, Classics Hair & Beauty, Kenilworth, England. Photography Simon Donnelly.

Curls can be increased on wavy hair by layering, which lessens weight and enables the hair to bounce up. By Gaylord Howlett for Schwarzkopf.

Naturally very tight curls need regular weekly intensive conditioning to keep hair glossy and tangle-free. The hair was misted with gel spray and diffuser-dried with the head held upside-down. By Lara Johnson, Mumbles, Swansea, Wales. Photography David Fernandez.

Above, left to right: Tonged and natural curls can be left loose and free or clipped up at random for these party looks. By Nick Wilding, La Vie en Rose, Cheshunt, Herts, England. Photography Mauro Cararro.

The hair was diffuser-dried with styling gel and each curl separated out into strands. The top hair was piled up and the rest left down. By Taryn MacGregor, London. Photography John Rowley.

Natural curls benefit from deep conditioning treats at least once a week. Conditioner is applied to shampooed hair, combed through and left to be absorbed for at least 10 minutes before rinsing. By Schumi, London.

Fine, wavy hair can look thicker and fuller if it is cut short like this. Styled with wet-look gel, the hair was simply arranged with fingers and left to dry naturally. By Taryn MacGregor, London. Photography John Rowley.

Permed hair was towel-dried, then wet-look gel was worked through before leaving hair to dry naturally. By Tina Shaw, Dimensions, Sheffield, England, for Goldwell.

A soft, texturizing perm gives lots of volume. Set hair on rollers and diffuser-dry or use a hood dryer. When cool, remove rollers, tilt head forward, mist with gel spray. By Sharon Malcolm, Hair Traffic, Belfast, N. Ireland.

Naturally curly hair can be styled smooth at the front and curly at the back, or curly all over. Mist with hairspray to hold the style. By Ian Robertson, Ian Robertson International, Kilmarnock, Scotland.

Fine highlights were woven through very curly hair to break up the texture. The hair was left to dry naturally, then finished by working serum through strands to give a polished finish. By Joseph and Jane Harling, Avon, England. Photography Barry Cook.

The hair was lightly permed, rough-dried, then set on medium-sized rollers and heat set. When the hair was dry, the rollers were removed and curls tousled. By L'Oréal Professionnel.

Curls were defined by diffuser-drying with styling spray, then tonging random individual curls to give separation. By Joseph and Jane Harling, Avon, England. Photography Barry Cook.

Lightly layered long hair was softly permed. After treatment, the hair can be roller set and left loose (*left*), partially swept up with tendrils flying (*far left*) or clipped up into a soft chignon (*middle*). By Keith Harris for Wella. Photography Sanders Nicolson.

THE SALON VISIT

London hairdresser, Nicky Clarke, always explains to his clients how to style their hair at home.

A professional cut is the basis of any style. Expert stylists evaluate your hair and lifestyle before they even pick up a pair of scissors. The best way to choose a salon is by personal recommendation. If a friend has a good haircut, ask them for the name of their hairdresser. If this is not possible you will have to do some research.

See if there are any salons in your area that look promising. Remember that the exterior can be deceptive, so have a look at the interior as well. The salon should be clean and welcoming, with a style and ambiance that appeals to you, and sales material that is new and fresh. The stylists should also reflect an image that you like.

THE FIRST VISIT

Once you have chosen a salon, make an appointment for a consultation. Wear clothes that reflect your lifestyle; for example, if you are a bank teller, don't wear a track-suit – you will give the stylist the wrong impression. Discuss your hair's idiosyncrasies and explain what you like and dislike about it. Spare a few minutes to discuss how you are going to manage the style between salon visits. If you want a wash-and-wear style that falls into place with the flick of a comb, say so. If you are prepared to spend 15 minutes a day scrunching a perm to perfection, then speak up.

Hairdressers are not mind-readers; neither can they wave a magic wand. However they can, with technical expertise, make the most of any type of hair. Listen to what they offer, but never be coerced into something with which you don't feel happy. Good hairdressers translate fashion trends into what is right for you. Yet you must be realistic; if your hair is thick and curly it will never hang in a straight, shiny bob, no matter how good the cut.

TAKING NOTES

While you are having your hair done, watch how your stylist does your hair, how much mousse or gel they apply and how they dry your hair. A good haircut should need the minimum of styling products and drying to achieve the desired result. Ask for advice on how to achieve the same look at home.

As a general rule, you need to have your hair cut every six to eight weeks, and to have a tint or colour regrowth every four weeks; a highlight root application needs to be done at least every three months, and perms every four to six months.

TECHNICAL SKILL

With such a wide variety of perms and colours available in chemists' shops, you may wonder why you should visit a salon to have your hair coloured or permed. Yet the fact is, that what you are buying is expertise and artistry. At the salon the stylist will use techniques that can be varied to suit the individual's specific hair textures and solve specific problems. For example, colours can be blended and applied in various ways to achieve a wide range of effects; hair can be made to look thicker and glossier by colour shading; perms can be used to give body, not just curl; long hair can be spiral or corkscrew-permed for movement; and special products can be used to refresh colours and reactivate curls.

COMPLAINTS

If you are not satisfied with the service you have received, then complain. Ask to see the salon manager, explain the problem, and ask what they are prepared to do about it. You should expect an apology, but don't expect to be offered a refund. If your hair has been badly permed, don't accept any offer to have it re-permed. The remedy is to have a course of intensive conditioning treatments. Following this, you should wait until the hair is in optimum condition before you have another perm or colour. If it is just a question of not liking the style, then that is a matter for discussion.

If you suffer serious damage, for example, an itchy, burning scalp, blisters, cuts, hair breakage or hair loss, then immediately seek advice from your family doctor or a trichologist. In the majority of cases, remedial treatment should be prescribed and the damage minimized. If the practitioner feels that you have cause for complaint and compensation, then the practitioner should prepare a report giving full details and an analysis of the problem. However, remember that hair grows, blisters heal, and memories fade. So, act quickly and, if necessary, make certain you have some photographs taken to reinforce your claim.

IMAGING

Imaging, which is available in some salons, is a means of previewing yourself on a video screen wearing a range of haircuts and colours. It is invaluable for experimenting with different looks before making a commitment to a particular style. Developed in France, the system is designed to take the stress out of choosing a style.

Watch how your stylist dries your hair. Here, Trevor Sorbie, London, lifts the front hair to create lift and movement.

AT THE SALON

Andrew Collinge at Andrew Collinge, Liverpool and Harrods, London, takes us through a salon visit. Follow his step-by-step guide to get a professional finish on your hair when you style at home.

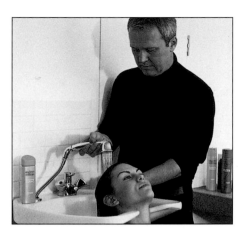

1 Andrew washes his model's hair with thickening shampoo, which creates fullness, before towelling off excess moisture.

2 Drying begins, using a round brush.

3 Thickening lotion is applied, concentrating application to the root area.

4 The head is tilted forward and thickening lotion applied to the crown area.

5 A smooth, volumized bob.

6 To get more volume, the model tilts her head forward and mists her hair with hairspray.

STYLING TOOLS AND TECHNIQUES

THERE ARE MANY DIFFERENT BRUSHES AND HEATED
STYLING EQUIPMENT THAT ENABLE YOU TO CHANGE
YOUR HAIR TEXTURE AND VOLUME.
ONCE YOU HAVE THE RIGHT EQUIPMENT FOR YOUR
HAIR YOU NEED TO MASTER STYLING IT. INVEST IN
THE BEST EQUIPMENT AND PRACTISE YOUR STYLING
TECHNIQUES TO GIVE YOUR HAIR THAT SALON FINISH
EVERY TIME YOU STYLE.

STYLING TOOLS

The right tools not only make hairstyling easier, but also make it more fun. Brushes, combs and pins are the basic tools of styling. The following is a guide to help you choose what is most suitable from the wide range that is available.

BRUSHES

Brushes are made of bristles (sometimes termed quills or pins), which may be natural hog bristle, plastic, nylon or wire. The bristles are embedded in a wooden, plastic or moulded rubber base and set in tufts or rows. This allows loose or shed hair to collect in the grooves without interfering with the action of the bristles. The spacing of the tufts plays an important role – generally, the wider the spacing between the rows of bristles the easier the brush will flow through the hair.

The role of brushing

Brushes help to remove tangles and knots and generally smooth the hair. The action of brushing from the roots to the ends removes dead skin cells and dirt, and encourages the cuticles to lie flat, thus reflecting the light. Brushing also stimulates the blood supply to the hair follicles, promoting healthy growth.

Natural bristles

Natural bristles are made of natural keratin (the same material as hair) and therefore create less friction and wear on the hair. They are good for grooming and polishing, and help to combat static on flyaway hair. However, they will not penetrate wet or thick hair and you must use a softer bristle brush for fine or thinning hair. In addition, the sharp ends can scratch the scalp.

> ### FACT FILE
>
> In the 17th century it was thought that brushing the hair would rid an individual of the vapours (fainting spells). However, women were advised not to groom their hair in the evening, as it could lead to headaches the next day. Hair brushes made from hog-bristle or hedgehog spines were first introduced in the late Middle Ages. With the invention of nylon in the 1930s designs changed, and now we can choose from an extensive range, each suitable for specific tasks.

> ### CLEANING
>
> All brushes should be cleaned by removing dead hairs and washing in warm, soapy water, then rinsing thoroughly. Natural bristle brushes should be placed bristle-side down and left to dry naturally. If you use a pneumatic brush with a rubber cushion base, block the air hole with a matchstick before washing.

Plastic, nylon or wire bristles

All of these bristles are easily cleaned and heat resistant, so they are good for blow-drying. They are available in a variety of shapes and styles. Cushioned brushes give good flexibility, as they glide through the hair, preventing tugging and helping to remove knots. They are also non-static.

A major disadvantage is that the ends can be harsh, so try to choose bristles with rounded or ball tips.

TYPES OF BRUSH

Circular or radial brushes come in a variety of sizes and are circular or semi-circular in shape. These brushes have either mixed bristles for finishing, a rubber pad with nylon bristles, or metal pins for styling. They are used to tame and control naturally curly, permed and wavy hair and are ideal for blow-drying. The diameter of the brush determines the resulting volume and movement, much the same way as rollers do.

Flat or half-round brushes are ideal for all aspects of wet or dry hairstyling and blow-drying. Normally they are made of nylon bristles in a rubber base. Some bases slide into position on to the plastic moulded handle. Rubber bases can be removed for cleaning and replacement bristles are sometimes available.

Pneumatic brushes have a domed rubber base with bristles set in tufts. They can be plastic, natural bristle or both.

Vent brushes have vented, hollow centres that allow the airflow from the dryer to pass through them. Special bristle, or pin patterns are designed to lift and disentangle even wet hair. Vents and tunnel brush heads enable the air to circulate freely through both the brush and the hair so the hair dries faster.

COMBS

Choose good quality combs with saw-cut teeth. This means that each individual tooth is cut into the comb, so there are no sharp edges. Avoid cheap, plastic combs that are made in a mould and so form lines down the centre of every tooth. They are sharp, and gradually scrape away the cuticle layers of the hair, causing damage and often breakage.

Use a wide-toothed comb for disentangling and combing conditioner through the hair. Fine tail-combs are for styling, Afro combs for curly hair, and styling combs for grooming.

PINS AND CLIPS

These are indispensable for sectioning and securing hair during setting, and for putting hair up. Most pins are available with untipped, plain ends, or cushion-tipped ends. Non-reflective finishes are available, so the pins are less noticeable in the hair, and most are made of metal, plastic or stainless steel. Colours include brown, black, grey, blonde, white and silver.

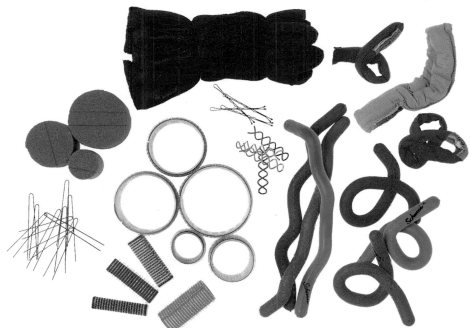

Double-pronged clips are most frequently used for making pin or barrel curls. Grips (pins) give security to curls, pleats (rolls) and all upswept styles. In North America they are known as "Bobbi" pins, in Britain as "Blendrites" and "Kirbis". To avoid discomfort, position grips (pins) in the hair so that the flat edge rests towards the scalp.

Heavy hairpins are made of strong metal and come either waved or straight. They are ideal for securing rollers and when putting hair up.

Fine hairpins are used for dressing hair. They are quite delicate and prone to bend out of shape, so they should only be used to secure small amounts of hair. These pins are easily concealed, especially if you use a matching colour. They are sometimes used to secure pin curls during setting, rather than using heavier clips, which can leave a mark.

Sectioning clips are clips with a single prong, and are longer in length than other clips. They are most often used for holding hair while working on another section, or securing pin curls.

Twisted pins are fashioned like a screw and are used to secure chignons and French pleats (rolls).

ROLLERS

Rollers vary in diameter, length and the material from which they are made.

Smooth rollers, that is, those without spikes or brushes, will give the sleekest finish, but are more difficult to put in. More popular are brush rollers, especially the self-holding variety that do not need pins or clips.

SHAPERS

Shapers were inspired by the principle of rag-rolling hair. Soft "twist tie" shapers are made from pliable rubber, plastic or cotton fabric and provide one of the more natural ways to curl hair. In the centre of each shaper is a tempered wire, which enables it to be bent into shape. The waves or curls that are produced are soft and bouncy and the technique is gentle enough for permed or tinted hair.

To use, section clean, dry hair and pull to a firm tension, "trapping" the end in a shaper that you have previously doubled over. Roll down to the roots of the hair and fold over to secure. Leave in for 30–60 minutes without heat, or for 10-15 minutes if you apply heat. If you twist the hair before curling you will achieve a more voluminous style.

STYLE EASY

The combination of practice and the right styling product enables you to achieve a salon finish at home. The products listed below enable you to do it in style.

GELS

Gels come in varying degrees of viscosity, from a thick jelly to a liquid spray. They are sometimes called sculpting lotions and are used for precise styling. Use them to lift roots, tame wisps, create tendrils, calm static, heat set, and give structure to curls. Wet gel can be used for sculpting styles.

> **TIP**
> A gel can be revitalized the following day by running wet fingers through the hair, against the direction of the finished look.

HAIR SPRAY

Traditionally, hairspray was used to hold a style in place; today, varying degrees of stiffness are available to suit all needs. Use hairspray to keep the hair in place, get curl definition when scrunching, and mist over rollers when setting.

Hairsprays are available in a variety of formulations, including light and firm holds. Photography by Silvikrin.

> **TIPS**
> ❍ A light application of spray on a hair brush can be used to tame flyaway ends.
> ❍ Use hairspray at the roots and tong or blow-dry the area to get immediate lift.

MOUSSE

Mousse is the most versatile styling product. It comes as a foam and can be used on wet or dry hair. Mousses contain conditioning agents and proteins to nurture and protect the hair. They are available in different strengths, designed to give soft to maximum holding power, and can be used to lift flat roots or smooth frizz. Use when blow-drying, scrunching and diffuser drying.

> **TIPS**
> ❍ Make sure you apply mousse from the roots to the ends, not just in a blob on the crown.
> ❍ Choose the right type for your hair. Normal is good for a great many styles, but if you want more holding power, don't just use more mousse as it can make hair dull; instead, choose a firm or maximum-hold product.

SERUMS

Serums, glossers, polishes and shine sprays are made from oils or silicones, which improve shine and softness by forming a microscopic film on the surface of the hair. Formulations can vary from light and silky to heavier ones with a distinct oily feel. They also contain substances designed to smooth the cuticle, encouraging the tiny scales to lie flat and thus reflect the light, and make the hair appear shiny. Use these products to improve the feel of the hair, to combat static, de-frizz, add shine and gloss, and temporarily repair split ends.

> **TIP**
> Don't use too much serum or you will make your hair greasy.

STYLING OR SETTING LOTIONS

Styling lotions contain flexible resins that form a film on the hair and aid setting, and protect the hair from heat damage. There are formulations for dry, coloured or sensitized hair; others give volume and additional shine. Use for roller-setting, scrunching, blow-drying and natural drying.

> **TIP**
> If using a styling lotion for heat setting, look out for formulations that offer thermal protection.

WAXES, POMADES AND CREAMS

These products are made from natural waxes, such as carnauba (produced by a Brazilian palm tree), which are softened with other ingredients such as mineral oils and lanolin to make them pliable. Both soft and hard formulations are available. Some pomades contain vegetable wax and oil to give gloss and sheen. Other formulations produce foam and are water soluble, and leave no residue. Use for dressing the hair and for controlling frizz and static.

When applying mousse use a "handful", and make sure you distribute it evenly. By Clynol.

APPLIANCES

Heated styling appliances allow you to style your hair quickly, efficiently and easily. A wide range of heated appliances is available.

AIR STYLERS

Air stylers combine the versatility of a hairdryer with the convenience of a styling wand. They operate on the same principle as a hairdryer, blowing warm air though the styler. Many stylers are available with a variety of clip-on options, including brushes, prongs and tongs, some with retractable teeth. Use for creating soft waves and volume at the roots.

TIP

Apply a styling spray or lotion before air styling and style the hair while it is still damp.

CRIMPERS

Crimpers consist of two ridged, metal plates that produce uniform patterned crimps in straight lines in the hair. The hair must be straightened first, either by blow-drying or using flat irons. The crimper is then used to give waves or ripples. Some crimpers have reversible or dual-effect styling plates to give different effects. Use for special styling effects or to increase volume.

TIPS

❍ Do not use on damaged, bleached or over-stressed hair.
❍ Brushing crimped hair gives a softer result.

HAIRDRYERS

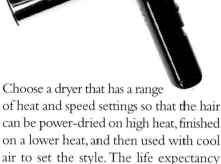

Choose a dryer that has a range of heat and speed settings so that the hair can be power-dried on high heat, finished on a lower heat, and then used with cool air to set the style. The life expectancy of a hairdryer averages between 200–300 hours. Use for blow-drying.

TIPS

❍ Always point the airflow down the hair shaft to smooth the cuticle and encourage shine.
❍ Take care not to hold the dryer too near the scalp; it can cause burns.
❍ When you have finished blow-drying, allow the hair to cool thoroughly, then check that the hair is completely dry. Warm hair often gives the illusion of dryness while it is, in fact, still damp.
❍ Never use a dryer without its filter in place – hair can easily be drawn into the machine.

The hairdryer is an essential piece of equipment, particularly when you need to dry your hair in a hurry. Photograph courtesy of BaByliss.

DIFFUSERS AND NOZZLES

Originally, diffusers were intended for drying curly hair slowly, to encourage curl formation for scrunched styles. The diffuser serves to spread the airflow over the hair so the curls are not blown away. The prongs on the diffuser head also help to increase volume at the root and give lift. Diffusers with flat heads are designed for gentle drying without ruffling, and are more suitable for shorter styles. The newest type of diffuser has long, straight prongs which are designed to inject

volume into straight hair while giving a smooth finish. Nozzles fit over the end of the barrel of the hairdryer and are used to give precise direction when styling.

HEATED ROLLERS

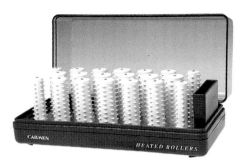

HOT BRUSHES

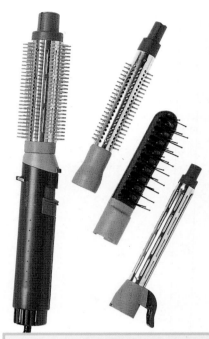

Heated rollers are available in sets and normally comprise a selection of around 20 small, medium and large rollers, with colour-coded clips to match. The early models came with spikes, which many women prefer because they have a good grip. New developments include ribbed rubber surfaces, which are designed to be kinder to the hair; curved barrel shapes that follow the form of the head and, more recently, clip fasteners.

The speed at which the rollers heat up varies, depending on the type of roller. PTC (positive temperature co-efficient) element rollers heat up fastest because they have an element inside each roller, and the heat is transferred directly from the base to the roller. Wax-filled rollers take longer, around 15 minutes, but they retain their temperature over a longer period. Most rollers cool down completely in 30 minutes. Use heated rollers for quick sets, to give curl and body. They are ideal for preparing long hair for dressing.

Hot brushes are easier to handle than tongs, and come in varying sizes for creating curls of different sizes. Wind down the length of the hair, hold for a few seconds until the heat has penetrated through the hair, then gently remove. Cordless hot brushes, which use butane cartridges or batteries to produce heat, are also available. Use for root lift, curl and movement.

When using a hot brush make certain you follow the manufacturer's instructions carefully. Photograph courtesy BaByliss.

STRAIGHTENERS

Straighteners, or flat irons, are based on the same principle as crimpers but have flat plates to iron out frizz or curl. Use for "pressing" really curly hair.

TIPS

❍ Use a styling spray before heat straightening.
❍ Straighteners are designed for occasional, not daily use, as they work at a high temperature, which can cause damage to the hair.

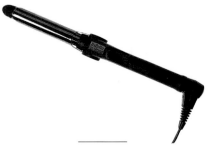

TONGS

Tongs consist of a barrel, or prong, and a depressor groove. The barrel is round; the depressor is curved to fit around the barrel when the tong is closed. The thickness of the barrel varies, and the size of the tong that is used depends on whether small, medium or large curls are required.

TIPS

❍ Be careful when tonging white or bleached hair as it can discolour.
❍ Always use tongs on dry, not wet, hair.
❍ If curling tight up to the roots, place a comb between the tongs and the scalp so the comb forms a barrier against the heat.
❍ Leave tonged curls to cool before styling.

TRAVEL DRYERS

Travel dryers are ideal for taking on holiday. They are usually miniature versions of standard dryers, and some are even available with their own small diffusers. Check that the dryer you buy has dual voltage and a travel case.

Keep holiday haircare to a minimum by making use of dual-purpose heated appliances. Don't forget to pack a universal plug when travelling to other countries. Photograph courtesy of Silvikrin.

SAFETY TIPS

❍ Equipment should be unplugged when not in use.
❍ Never use electric equipment with wet hands, and don't use near water.
❍ Use only one appliance for each socket outlet – adaptors may cause overload.
❍ The cord should not be wrapped tightly around the equipment; coil it loosely before storing.
❍ Tongs can be cleaned by wiping with a damp cloth; if necessary, use a little methylated spirits to remove dirt.
❍ All electrical equipment should be checked periodically to ensure that leads and connections are in good order.
❍ Untwist the cord on the dryer from time to time.
❍ Clean filters regularly – a blocked filter means the dryer has to work harder and will eventually overheat and cut out. If the element overheats it can distort the dryer casing.

BLOW-DRYING LONG HAIR

By following our step-by-step instructions you can achieve the smoothest, sleekest blow-dry ever.

1 Shampoo and condition your hair.

5 Using your other hand, spread the mousse through the hair, distributing it evenly from the tips to the ends.

STYLING CHECKLIST

You will need:
✔ styling comb
✔ dryer
✔ mousse
✔ clip
✔ styling brush
✔ serum

2 Comb through with a wide-toothed comb to remove any tangles.

3 Partially dry your hair to remove excess moisture.

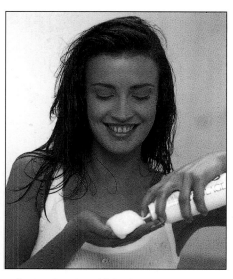

4 Apply a handful of mousse to the palm of your hand.

6 Divide your hair into two main sections by clipping the top and sides out of the way. Then, working on the hair that is left free and taking one small section at a time, hold the dryer in one hand and a styling brush in the other. Place the brush underneath the first section of hair, positioning it at the roots. Keeping the tension on the hair taut (but without undue stress), move the brush down towards the ends, directing the air flow from the dryer so that it follows the downward movement of the brush.

7 Curve the brush under at the ends to achieve a slight bend. Concentrate on drying the root area first, repeatedly introducing the brush to the roots once it has moved down the length of the hair. Continue the movement until the first section of the hair is dry. Repeat for the other sections until the whole of the back section is completely dry.

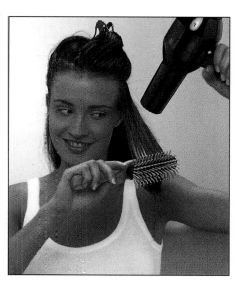

8 Release a section of hair from the top and dry it in the same manner. Continue in this way until you have dried all your hair. Finish by smoothing a few drops of serum through the hair to flatten any flyaway ends.

TIPS
❍ Use the highest heat or speed setting to remove excess moisture, then switch to medium to finish drying.
❍ Point the airflow downwards. This smoothes the cuticles and makes the hair shine.
❍ When blow-drying, make sure each section is completely dry before going to the next.

FINGER DRYING

This is a quick method of drying and styling your hair. It relies on the heat released from your hands rather than the heat from a dryer. Finger drying is suitable for short to mid-length hair.

1 Shampoo and condition your hair, then spray with gel and comb through.

2 Run your fingers rapidly upwards and forwards, from the roots to the ends.

> **TIP**
> Finger drying is the best way to dry damaged hair, or to encourage waves in naturally curly, short hair.

STYLING CHECKLIST

You will need:
✔ spray gel
✔ styling comb

3 Lift up the hair at the crown to get height at the roots.

4 Continue lifting as the hair dries. Use your fingertips to flatten the hair at the sides.

BARREL CURLS

One of the simplest sets is achieved by curling the hair around the fingers and then pinning the curl in place. Barrel curls create a soft set.

1 Shampoo and condition your hair; apply setting lotion and comb through from the roots to the ends. Take a small section of hair (about 2.5 cm/ 1 in) and smooth it upwards.

2 Loop the hair into a large curl.

3 Clip in place.

> **STYLING CHECKLIST**
>
> *You will need:*
> ✔ setting lotion
> ✔ styling comb
> ✔ clips
> ✔ hood dryer (optional)
> ✔ hair brush (optional)

4 Continue to curl the rest of the hair in the same way.

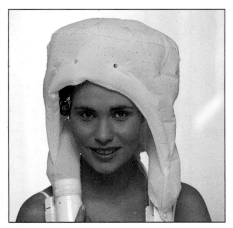

5 Dry the hair with a hood dryer, or allow it to dry naturally. Remove the clips. To achieve a tousled look, rake your fingers through your hair. For a smoother finish use a hair brush.

ROLL-UP

TIPS
❍ Use large diameter rollers for sleek, wavy looks, smaller rollers for curlier styles.
❍ Always use sections of equal width when setting the hair or you will get an uneven result.
❍ For maximum volume and control, let the hair cool completely before brushing through.
❍ A bristle brush will give a smoother finish to the style.
❍ If the finished set is too curly after brushing through, loosen the curl with a brush used with a hand dryer.
❍ To create extra volume and height use a fine-toothed comb to backcomb the roots.

A roller set forms the basis of many styles; it can be used to smooth hair, add waves or soft curls, or provide a foundation for an upswept style.

1 Shampoo and condition your hair, then partially dry to remove excess moisture. Mist with a styling spray.

2 For a basic set, take a 5 cm/2 in section of hair (or a section the same width as your roller) from the centre front and comb it straight up, smoothing out any tangles.

3 Wrap the ends of the sectioned hair around the roller, taking care not to buckle the hair. Then wind the roller down firmly, towards the scalp, keeping the tension even.

4 Keep winding until the roller sits on the roots of the hair. Self-holding rollers will stay in place on their own, but if you are using brush rollers you will have to fasten them with a pin.

5 Continue around the whole head, always taking the same width of hair. Re-mist the hair with styling spray if it begins to dry out.

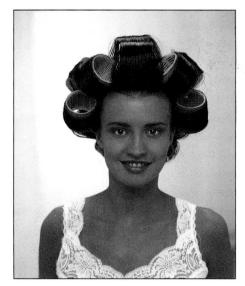

6 Leave the finished set to dry naturally, or dry it with a diffuser attachment on your hand dryer, or with a hood dryer. When using artificial heat sources, allow the completely dry hair to become quite cool before you remove the rollers. Brush through the hair following the direction of the set. Mist the brush with hairspray and use to smooth any stray hairs.

SOFT SETTING

Fabric rollers are the modern version of old-fashioned rags. Apart from being very easy to use, they are kind to the hair and give a highly effective set.

1 Dampen the hair with styling spray, making sure you distribute it evenly from the roots to the ends.

5 Leave the completed set to dry naturally.

TIP
For even more volume, twist each section of hair lengthwise before winding it on to the fabric roller.

3 Continue winding the roller right down to the roots.

2 Using sections of hair about 2.5 cm/ 1 in wide, curl the end of the hair around a fabric roller and wind the roller down towards the scalp, taking care not to buckle the ends of the hair.

6 When the hair is dry, remove the rollers by unbending the ends and unwinding the hair.

7 When all the rollers have been removed, the hair falls into firm corkscrew curls.

4 To fasten, simply bend each end of the fabric roller towards the centre. This grips the hair and holds it in place.

8 Working on one curl at a time, rake your fingers through the hair, teasing out each curl. The result will be a full, voluminous finish.

STYLE AND GO

Heated gas stylers with brush and tong attachments enable you to create lots of styles. Here we show you two different techniques, which give two different looks.

STYLING CHECKLIST

You will need:
✔ styling lotion
✔ heated gas styler with brush and tong attachment
✔ clips

1 Shampoo, condition, and dry your hair.

2 Take a section of hair about 5 cm/ 2 in square and apply some styling lotion. Using the brush attachment on the styler, gently smooth the hair from the roots to the ends. Place the styler near the roots, twist the hair around the brush, and hold for a few seconds. Gently unravel the hair and hold without pulling.

3 Place the ends of the hair into the styler and wind halfway down the hair length.

4 Unwind and loop the hair into a barrel curl, securing with a clip. Repeat steps 2 to 4 until you have done the whole head. Remove the clips. Comb.

1 Shampoo, condition and dry your hair.

3 Continue wrapping the hair down the length of the barrel, taking care not to buckle the ends of the hair. Hold for a few seconds to allow the curl to form.

4 Release the depressor and allow the spiral curl to spring out. Repeat steps 2 to 3 until you have curled the whole head, then rake through the hair with your fingers for a softly tousled look.

Use the tong attachment for a tousled look.

2 Take a section of hair about 1 cm/ ½ in long and apply some styling lotion. Using the tong attachment on the styler, lift the depressor and keep it open. Slide the tongs on to the hair, just up from the roots. Holding the depressor open, wind the hair around the barrel, towards the face, ensuring the ends are smooth.

TIP
After tonging the hair, don't be tempted to brush your hair or you will lose the curl.

Hair by Keith Harris
using Braun styling appliances.
Photography Iain Philpott.

STYLING TRICKS
❍ Always use heated gas stylers on dry hair, never on wet hair.
❍ Don't use mousse or gel when heat styling. Instead, try special heat-activated styling lotions and sprays. These are designed to help curls hold their shape without making the hair sticky or frizzy.
❍ Bobbed styles can be smoothed down and the ends of the hair tipped under using a heated gas styler. Just section the hair and smooth the tongs down the length, curving the ends. It is important to keep the tongs moving with a gentle sliding action, twisting the wrist and turning the barrel of the tongs under.
❍ Unruly fringes (bangs) can be tamed by gently winding the fringe around the tong or styler and holding for a few seconds.

TONG AND TWIST

Tongs can also be used to smooth the hair and add just the right amount of movement.

1 Shampoo, condition and dry your hair. Apply a mist of styling lotion. Never use mousse as it will stick to the tongs and bake into the hair. Divide off a small section of hair.

STYLING CHECKLIST

You will need:
✔ styling lotion
✔ styling comb
✔ tongs

2 Press the depressor to open the tongs.

3 Wind the section of hair around the barrel of the tongs.

4 Release the depressor to hold the hair in place and wait a few seconds for the curl to form. Remove the tongs and leave the hair to cool while you work on the rest of the hair. Style by raking through with your fingers.

TIP
Never use tongs on bleached hair. The high heat can damage the hair, causing brittleness and breakage.

AIRWAVES

Air styling makes use of gentle heat and combines it with the moisture in your hair to give a long-lasting curl.

1 Shampoo and condition your hair. Mist with styling lotion.

3 Clip on the tong attachment and continue shaping the hair by wrapping it around the tongs.

4 Repeat steps 2 and 3 until the whole head is curled and waved. When the hair is completely dry, rake your fingers through it.

2 Using the brush attachment on the styler, start drying the hair. Lift each section to allow the heat to dry the roots.

STYLING CHECKLIST

You will need:
✔ styling lotion
✔ air styler with brush and tong attachment

TIP
Switch your air styler to low speed for more controlled styling and finishing.

CURL CREATION

Naturally wavy hair can be scrunched into beautiful curls using this diffuser-drying technique.

1 The hair has natural movement that needs to be encouraged to form into waves and curls.

2 Shampoo, condition and towel-dry your hair, then use a wide-toothed comb to untangle from roots to ends.

3 Apply mousse, distributing it evenly and working well into the hair with your hands.

4 Clip the top section of hair out of the way for a moment. Attach the diffuser to the dryer and dry the lower hair. This action enables the warm air to circulate around the strands of hair, which encourages the formation of curls. To maximize the amount of curl, use your hands to scrunch up handfuls of hair.

5 Unclip the top section. Tip head sideways and allow the hair to sit in the diffuser cup. Do not pull the hair, simply squeeze curls gently into shape.

6 Tilt head forwards to complete the drying process. Do not forget to aim heat on the nape of the neck as well, before lifting head up and arranging curls.

> **TIP**
> This technique works equally well on permed hair, giving separation and definition to curls and waves.

SMOOTH AND STRAIGHT

Volume can be added to long, straight hair by using a dryer with a diffuser attachment that has long, straight prongs.

2 Shampoo and condition your hair, then part it down the centre. Attach a diffuser with long prongs to your dryer and as the hair dries, comb the prongs down the hair in a stroking movement. This will direct the airflow downwards, smoothing and separating the hair.

1 Long, thick hair often tangles easily and it is difficult to add volume and control.

3 To create volume at the top and sides, slide the prongs through the hair to the roots at the crown, then gently rotate the diffuser. Repeat until you have achieved maximum volume.

Photograph courtesy of Braun.
Appliance, Braun Supervolume.

INSTANT SET

Hair can be given lift, bounce, and movement with a quick set using heated rollers.

1 Shampoo and condition your hair. Apply mousse and blow-dry smooth. Heat the rollers according to the manufacturer's instructions.

2 Wind sections of hair (about 5 cm/ 2in wide) on to a roller, taking care not to buckle the ends of the hair. Use medium and small rollers at the front and sides, larger rollers on the crown.

3 Wind the rollers down towards the root, making sure that the ends are tucked under smoothly. Keep the tension even. Secure each roller with the clip supplied. Mist your set hair with a styling lotion. Allow the rollers to cool completely and then remove them, taking care not to disturb the curl too much. To finish, loosen the curls by raking your fingers through them.

Hair by Trevor Sorbie, London.

STYLING CHECKLIST

You will need:
✔ mousse
✔ dryer
✔ heated rollers
✔ styling lotion

TIP
A heated roller set forms the foundation for many styles and is a simple way to restyle the hair.

CRIMPING CRAZY

If you use a crimper with a choice of styling plates, you can devise a variety of looks that add instant ripples and waves to your hair.

1 This first step forms the basis for all the crimping styles. Before you begin, shampoo and condition your hair, then blow-dry it straight and mist with a styling lotion. Fit the styling plate of your choice to the crimper, following the manufacturer's directions. Working on one section of hair at a time, hold the hot crimper on your hair for a few seconds and then release. Move down the hair and apply the crimper again. Make sure that you line up the crimping plates carefully to ensure a uniform effect. Repeat to the end of the section of hair, then work around your head in the same way.

Left: For this crimped style, use the wave-making plates over the whole head.

All hairstyles on these two pages by Charles Worthington for BaByliss.

2 Use the standard crimping plates to give texture and volume to your hair, then section off the top hair into a ponytail and slip two bun rings over it. Finally, fan out random sections of hair and hold with firm-hold hairspray for a fun look.

3 Create a shimmer by using a crimping plate with a fine ridge. This not only adds texture to the hair, but also makes the hair look more shiny. Simply crimp the top sections of your hair at random. The effect can be used on long hair or hair cut in a bob.

4 For a slightly softer crimp, after shampooing and conditioning, work some gel mousse through your hair before you dry it. This will help give it body. Then use the deep wave plates to create waves. Finally, ruffle through your hair using a wide-toothed comb to add more volume and softness.

> **TIP**
> Don't use crimpers on bleached hair as the high heat needed to crimp the hair can cause drying and splitting.

5 Achieve this "bamboo" effect by crimping the hair in fine sections to produce a very crisp, definite effect. Starting at the roots, crimp down a section at a time, working as evenly as possible. When you have finished, leave the hair in crimped sections, do not brush it through. Finally, secure a bun ring to the top of the head and pin the hair on to it in swirls, leaving a few lengths of hair sweeping down at the front to soften the style.

ALL-OVER CRIMP

1 Straight hair is shampooed, conditioned and roughly blow-dried straight.

Long, straight hair can be totally transformed by crimping.

2 Clip top hair out of the way and apply hairspray to one section of hair.

3 Hold the hot crimper on this section of your hair for a few seconds and then release. Move down the hair and apply the crimper again. Make sure that you line up the crimping plates carefully to ensure a uniform effect. Repeat to the end of the section of hair.

STYLING CHECKLIST

You will need:
✔ section clip
✔ hairspray
✔ crimper with deep-wave plates
✔ wide-toothed comb

4 Continue crimping sections of hair in the same way – here you see one side of the hair completely crimped.

5 Crimp the other side in the same way, then lightly loosen the crimp by running a wide-toothed comb through the outer layers of hair.

SECTION CRIMP

Crimping just a section of hair
gives a different look
in minutes.

1 Long hair has a slight natural wave.

2 Blow-dry a section at a time using a smoothing attachment on the hairdryer.

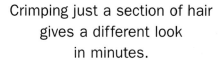

3 Smooth back hair in the same way.

4 All the hair is now smooth and straight.

STYLING CHECKLIST

You will need:
✔ dryer with smoother attachment
✔ crimper with deep-wave plate
✔ butterfly slide (barrette)

5 Crimp one section of hair, holding the hot crimper in place for a few seconds before releasing. Move down the hair and apply the crimper again. Make sure that you line up the crimping plates carefully to ensure a uniform effect all the way down each section of hair. Finish by clipping a butterfly slide (barrette) in place.

ROOT CRIMP

STYLING CHECKLIST

You will need:
✔ hairspray
✔ crimper with medium-wave plate
✔ section clip

Mid-length hair can be given lots of volume by crimping the roots.

1 Straight, layered hair is shampooed, conditioned and rough-dried.

2 Take a section of hair from the crown and apply hairspray.

3 Hold hair between the plates of the crimper for a few seconds, then release.

TIP
For a smoother look, with lots of root volume, simply brush hair through with a bristle brush.

4 The first section of hair is crimped. For this look you only need to crimp the root section of hair, not the entire length.

5 Work in this manner all over the head, clipping previously crimped hair out of the way.

6 The crimping is completed. To finish, tilt your head back and smooth the hair with your fingers.

BLOW-DRYING SHORT HAIR

Smooth short hair into this sleek and shiny style following the step-by-step guide.

1 Shampoo and condition your hair, then work mousse through from the roots to ends.

2 Dry one section of hair at a time using the brush from underneath to smooth.

3 Continue working in the same manner all round the head.

STYLING CHECKLIST

You will need:
✔ mousse
✔ hairdryer
✔ styling brush
✔ finishing cream or wax

4 Smooth any frizziness and give hair texture by working a little finishing cream or wax through the hair.

For a more tousled look, ruffle the hair with your fingers.

RUFFLE-DRYING

This is a simple technique that achieves lots of volume on short hair.

1 Shampoo and condition your hair, then work mousse through from the roots to ends.

2 Use your fingers to ruffle the hair as it dries, concentrating the dryer on the roots.

3 Finish drying the ends of the hair.

4 Mist with hairspray to hold the style.

STYLING CHECKLIST

You will need:
✔ mousse
✔ dryer
✔ hairspray

DIFFUSER-DRYING

Short, straight hair can be quickly dried with a diffuser attachment.

1 Shampoo and condition hair, then work styling cream through.

2 Comb hair to distribute the styling cream.

3 Use the diffuser attachment and dryer set on a low heat and speed to dry hair – it should only take a few minutes.

STYLING CHECKLIST

You will need:
✔ styling cream
✔ styling comb
✔ dryer with diffuser attachment

STRAIGHTENING

Flat irons can be used to smooth out waves and frizz in double-quick time.

1 The hair is shampooed, conditioned and left to dry naturally. Clip top hair out of the way and, working on a section of hair at a time, use flat irons to smooth hair downwards.

STYLING CHECKLIST

You will need:
✔ section clip
✔ flat irons
✔ hairspray
✔ serum

2 Continue in this manner until all the hair is smoothed.

3 Once you have finished straightening, mist with hairspray to help prevent frizzing.

4 A few drops of serum worked through the hair prevents static and any tendency to fly away.

VOLUMISING

Naturally wavy hair can be given volume and controlled curl.

1 Shampoo and towel-dry hair to remove excess moisture, then begin drying using the hot styling brush with the flat brush attachment.

2 Create lift on the crown area by winding hair round the barrel of the hot styling brush with the round brush attachment.

3 Continue working in the same manner, flicking the ends out.

4 Give separation and texture to the ends by working through just a little styling cream.

FLICKING

Straight hair can be given smoothness and just a little curl or wave.

1 Shampoo, condition and rough-dry hair. Clip up top hair and work on one section at a time, running flat irons down the hair and flicking the ends out slightly.

2 Work on the crown hair in the same way.

3 Smooth the fringe (bangs), keeping it as straight as possible.

4 Work a little wax through the lengths and ends of hair for separation and texture.

STYLING CHECKLIST

You will need:
✔ section clip
✔ flat irons
✔ wax

STEAM SETTING

Steam-activated foam rollers give a quick and easy instant set that produces lots of movement and soft curl.

1 Heat up one foam roller at a time following the directions supplied by the manufacturer.

4 Repeat all over the head until all the hair is wound on rollers.

3 Fix the roller, using one of the clips supplied.

2 Take one section of hair and wind the roller downwards from the ends to the scalp, taking care to keep the hair taut.

TIP
Steam works by gently softening the inner structure of the hair, allowing it to re-form in the shape of the roller. Always make sure that the rollers are completely cool before removing or your set will drop.

5 When your hair is completely cool remove rollers, one a time, allowing the hair to fall free. Lightly brush into waves and soft curls.

ALL-OVER TONGING

Straight hair can be transformed into a mass of curls by tonging. It takes a little practice, but the result is well worth the time.

1 The hair is shampooed and conditioned before rough-drying.

5 One half of the hair is tonged.

TIP
For a softer look the following day, use a bristle brush to smooth hair into soft waves.

2 Clip top hair out of the way, then take one section of hair at the side and mist with styling spray.

3 Open the depressor on the tongs and wind the section of hair round the barrel, taking care not to buckle the ends. Hold the hair with the depressor in place for a few minutes to set the curl.

4 Continue in this manner, completing each curl before moving on to the next.

6 Repeat on other side to complete the tonging.

7 Use your fingers to gently release tension in the curls. Do not brush or you will lose the curl.

8 Tilt your head forward and mist with spray to finish, then flick the hair back.

PARTIAL TONGING

This is a super-quick way to transform straight hair with just a few pretty curly tendrils.

STYLING CHECKLIST

You will need:
✔ tongs
✔ serum

1 Open the depressor on the tongs and wind one section of hair round the barrel, taking care not to buckle the ends.

2 Hold the hair with the depressor in place for a few minutes to set the curl. Repeat all over the head.

3 Work a few drops of serum through each curl to give smoothness.

FINGER WAVING

Soft waves add a sophisticated look to long hair.

1 Shampoo, condition and rough-dry the hair.

2 Comb liquid styling gel through the front section of hair.

3 Form a wave by using both styling combs to form an S-shape.

4 Hold the wave in place with a hair slide (barrette) then make another wave in the same way and hold in place with more slides clipped close together.

STYLING CHECKLIST

You will need:
- ✔ liquid styling gel
- ✔ styling combs
- ✔ slides (barrettes)

VOLUME SETTING

STYLING CHECKLIST

You will need:
- ✔ mousse
- ✔ flat irons
- ✔ self-holding rollers
- ✔ hairspray
- ✔ styling comb

Even the straightest hair can be given volume and height by quick setting.

1 The hair is shampooed, conditioned and left until nearly dry.

5 Mist hair with hairspray.

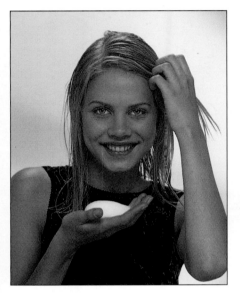

2 Mousse is applied from the roots to the ends.

3 Take one section on the crown and smooth upwards with flat irons.

4 Wind hair on to a self-holding roller, taking care not to buckle the ends. This type of roller needs no pins or clips as the Velcro holds it in place.

6 Wind the rest of the hair in the same manner, then mist again with hairspray.

7 Remove the rollers one at a time and allow hair to fall free.

8 When all the rollers are removed, mist the roots with hairspray once again to hold the volume, then comb into place.

HEATED STYLES

This type of heated styler enables you to create beautiful curls on long hair and is especially effective if the hair has a few layers.

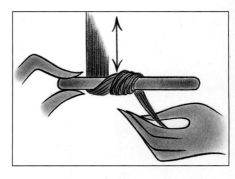

1 To begin winding, take a section of hair and comb straight, holding it taut with one hand.

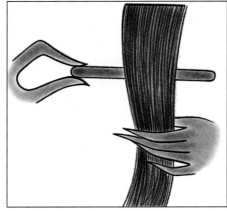

3 Now take the hair and wind it round the styler all in one movement. It is important not to let go of the hair.

2 Place the pre-heated styler parallel across the inside of the section approximately 5 cm/2 in from the roots, as shown. There should be 2.5 cm/1 in of styler on one side of the section of hair, the rest on the other side.

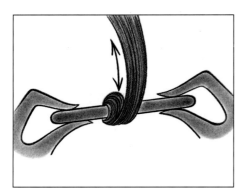

4 Holding the ends of the styler, unwind a little and then rewind up so you trap the ends of the hair and stop it from unravelling.

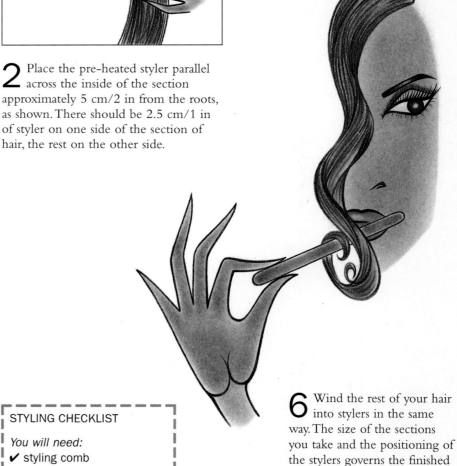

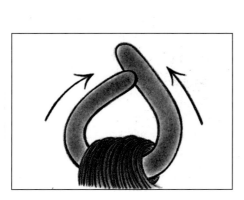

5 Secure by folding the ends of the styler over as shown.

STYLING CHECKLIST

You will need:
✔ styling comb
✔ set of flexi-stylers
✔ pure bristle brush
✔ spray serum
✔ wide-toothed comb
✔ wax
✔ hairspray

6 Wind the rest of your hair into stylers in the same way. The size of the sections you take and the positioning of the stylers governs the finished result. See illustrations which show how to position your stylers to re-create the style you require. Leave the stylers until they are completely cool before removing, one at a time, taking care not to tangle hair.

Hair Nicky Clarke, London

Hollywood Glamour

To achieve smooth results it is essential that you work cleanly and neatly. Starting from a side parting, take 7.5 cm/ 3 in-wide sections. Drag hair down flat to the head, and wind on to the stylers, positioning the remaining stylers as shown to achieve sleek waves. Leave the stylers until completely cool, then remove and smooth the hair using a pure bristle brush. Mist with spray serum to give extra gloss.

Pre-Raphaelite Curls

Work straight back from the hairline and divide hair into small sections – each approximately 2.5 cm/1 in wide. Wind hair on to stylers following the step-by-step guide. Position the stylers as shown to achieve masses of tight curls. Leave until completely cool, then unwind the hair from one styler at a time and use the fingers or a wide-toothed comb to gently separate each curl. Remove the remaining stylers, then work a little wax through each curl to give separation and definition.

Soft Tumbling Curls

Work straight back from the hairline and divide hair into medium sections – each approximately 5 cm/2 in wide. The illustration shows how to position the stylers to achieve lots of loose curls. Leave until completely cool, then remove the stylers one at a time. Tilt your head forward and use a wide-toothed comb to gently separate the hair, starting at the ends and working towards the roots. Tilt your head up again and mist with hairspray to give a soft, lasting hold.

Illustrations: Emil Nair

MEET THE EXPERT

International stylist Trevor Sorbie, four times holder of the British Hairdresser of the Year Award, uses scrunching and other techniques to create these award-winning looks. His favourite tip is: "Let your fingers do the styling."

Thick, wavy hair like this model's tends to go frizzy and dull if left to dry naturally. Follow Trevor Sorbie's step-by-step guide to produce these beautiful results.

STYLING CHECKLIST

You will need:
For scrunching:
✔ section grips (pins)
✔ styling spray
✔ dryer with diffuser attachment
✔ soft wax
For fingerwaving:
✔ sculpting gel
✔ styling comb

1 Brush the hair off the face and then push the front hair forwards into waves. Secure the waves with a row of section grips and then apply a curl-forming spray.

2 Use the diffuser attachment on your dryer to gently lift the curls. Dry the roots from underneath first, to help encourage lift and volume. When the hair is completely dry, run your fingers through the hair to give definition. For extra texture and separation, use a little soft wax, rubbing it between the palms of your hands first to warm it, then apply it to the ends of the curls with your fingertips.

To create a completely different look, the hair is skilfully styled using finger-waving techniques.

1 Shampoo and condition your hair. Towel dry to remove excess moisture, then apply a small amount of sculpting gel. Don't apply the gel directly from the bottle; dispense some on to the palm of your hand first.

2 Spread the gel on to the hair a little at a time, using your other hand to sculpt the hair into waves.

3 Part the hair in the centre, then comb down smooth from the temples, as shown. Leave the ends around the hairline to curl freely. Use a comb with widely spaced teeth to shape the hair into waves, using your fingers and comb to create S-shapes. Allow to dry naturally or, if you are in a hurry, use a flat diffuser, which dries without ruffling the hair.

Hair Trevor Sorbie, London.

HAIR DRESSING

ONCE YOU HAVE MASTERED THE BASIC HAIR SETTING
AND DRYING TECHNIQUES, YOU CAN USE THESE SKILLS
AS THE FOUNDATION FOR DRESSING YOUR HAIR IN
MANY DIFFERENT STYLES. OUR SPECIAL PROJECTS
SHOW YOU HOW TO CREATE BRAIDS, CHIGNONS,
FRENCH PLEATS (ROLLS), TOP KNOTS, TWISTS, COILS
AND CURLS. BY FOLLOWING THE SIMPLE STEP-BY-STEP
GUIDES, YOU CAN RE-CREATE THE LOOKS EXACTLY.
YOU'LL BE AMAZED HOW EASY IT IS TO TRANSFORM
TOTALLY YOUR HAIR TO SUIT ALMOST
EVERY MOOD AND OCCASION.

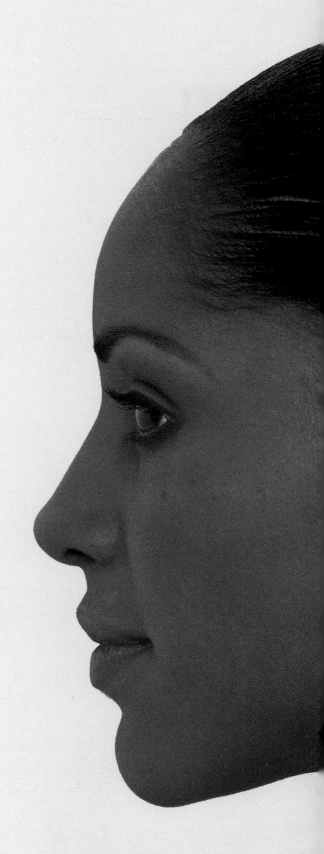

TWIST AND BRAID

Add interest to a classic style
by twisting the sides of the hair
and then weaving them
into a braid.

2 Secure the twist with a hair pin at the nape of the neck, then repeat these two steps on the other side.

1 Take a small section of hair on one side of your head, just above your ear, and divide it into two equal strands. Start twisting the two strands of hair together. Continue twisting downwards, towards the ends of the hair.

3 Next, incorporate the twisted sections into a basic three-stranded braid. To braid, simply split the hair into three equal strands, taking the twisted sections into the left and right strands. Then bring the right strand over the centre strand, the left strand over the centre, and then the right over the centre again. Continue in this manner to the end. Finally, secure the end with a covered band and decorate with a clip bow.

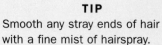

TIP
Smooth any stray ends of hair
with a fine mist of hairspray.

DRAGGED SIDE BRAIDS

Curly hair can be controlled, yet still allowed to flow free, by braiding at the sides and allowing the hair at the back to fall in a mass of curls.

1 Part your hair in the centre and divide off a large section at the side, combing it as flat as possible to the head.

2 Divide the section into three equal strands and hold them apart.

3 Begin to make a dragged braid by pulling the strands of hair towards your face and then braiding in the normal way, that is, taking the right strand over the centre strand, the left strand over the centre, and the right over the centre again, keeping the braid in the position shown.

4 Continue braiding to the end and secure the end with a covered band. Tuck the braid behind your ear and pin it in place, then make a second braid on the other side.

TIP
Encourage curls to form by spraying the hair with water and then scrunching with your hands.

STYLING CHECKLIST

Time: 5 minutes
Ease/difficulty: Easy
Hair type: Long and naturally curly or permed

You will need:
✔ styling comb
✔ covered bands
✔ hair grips (pins)

PRETTY BRAID

Straight hair is smoothed to perfection, then enhanced with a tiny braided bow.

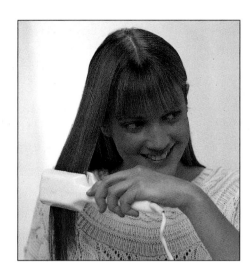

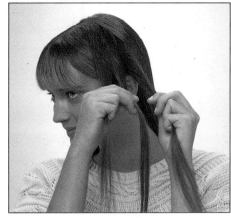

1 Part your hair in the centre and, taking one section of hair at a time, run straightening irons from the roots to the tips to smooth out any kinks.

2 On one side of the head, midway along the centre parting, pick up a small section of hair and comb it straight. Divide this section into three strands and braid the hair.

3 Continue in this way to the end, and then secure with a small covered band. Make a second braid on the other side of your head.

4 Finally, tie the braids in a bow at the centre back of your head, as shown. Secure with pins and decorate the ends by binding them with fine ribbon.

STYLING CHECKLIST

Time: 10 minutes
Ease/difficulty: Quite easy
Hair type: Long, slightly wavy, or straight

You will need:
✔ straightening irons
✔ styling comb
✔ small covered bands
✔ hairpins
✔ short length of fine ribbon

RIBBON BOW

A simple ponytail is given added interest by binding with ribbon and finishing with a bow.

1 Brush your hair smoothly back into a neat ponytail, leaving a small section at either side free. Secure the ponytail with a covered band.

2 Position the centre of the ribbon over the band as shown, pulling the ends of the ribbon taut.

3 Cross the ribbon over the ponytail.

4 Continue crossing the ribbon around the ponytail in the same manner until you are 5–7.5 cm/2–3 in from the end. Tie the ribbon into a bow. Smooth out the side sections of hair and tie them into a neat bow at the centre-back of your head above the beribboned ponytail. Secure with a pin if necessary.

STYLING CHECKLIST

Time: 5 minutes
Ease/difficulty: Easy
Hair type: Long and straight

You will need:
✔ brush
✔ covered band
✔ about 1 m/1 yd of ribbon
✔ hairpin

PONYTAIL STYLER

A simple ponytail can be transformed easily and quickly using this clever styler.

TIP
To smooth any flyaway ends, rub a few drops of serum in the palms of your hands and smooth over the hair.

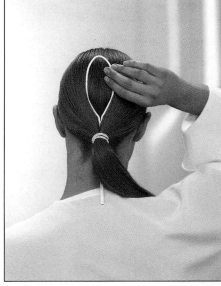

1 Clasp the hair into a ponytail and secure it with a covered band. Insert the styler as shown.

2 Thread the ponytail through the styler.

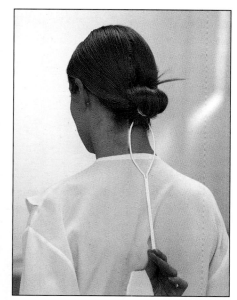

5 ... so the ponytail pulls through ...

3 Begin to pull the styler down ...

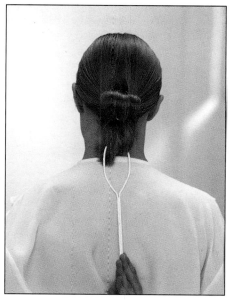

6 ... and emerges underneath.

4 continue pulling ...

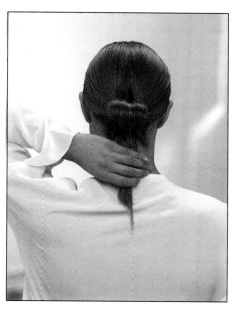

7 Smooth the hair with your hand and insert the styler again, repeating steps 2 to 6 once more to give a neat and smooth, chignon loop.

CURLY STYLER

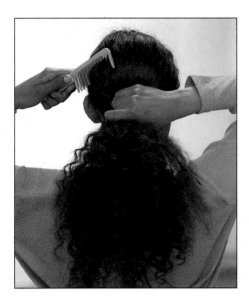

The ponytail styler can also be used to tame a mass of curls, creating a ponytail with a simple double twist.

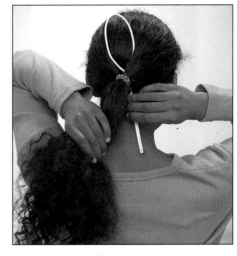

1 Use a comb with widely spaced teeth to smooth the hair back and into a ponytail. Secure with a covered band.

2 Insert the styler as shown.

3 Thread the ponytail through the styler.

Side view of finished style.

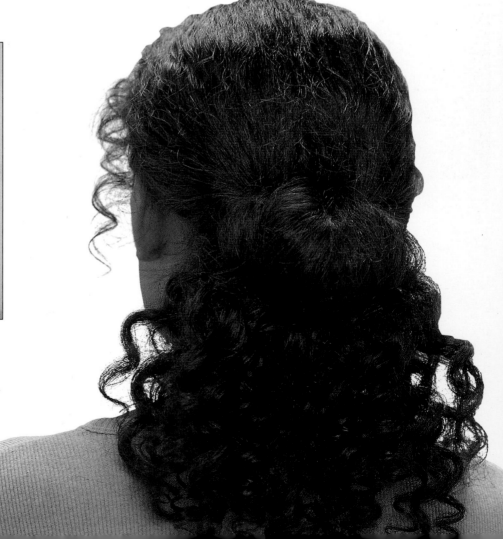

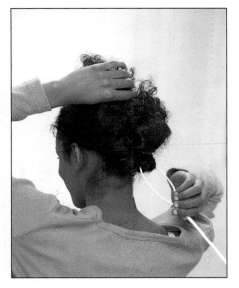

4 Begin to pull the styler down ...

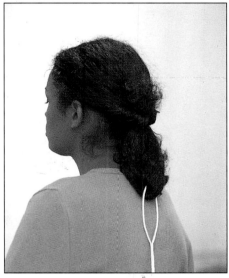

5 ... continue pulling ...

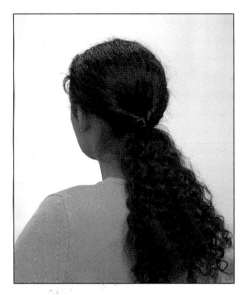

6 ... so that the ponytail pulls through.

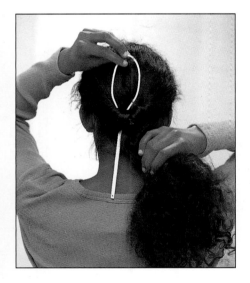

7 Repeat steps 3 to 6.

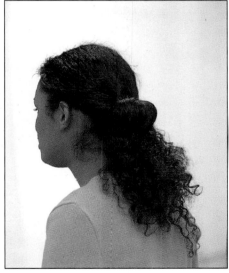

8 Apply a little mousse to your hands and use it to reform the curls, scrunching to achieve a good shape.

STYLING CHECKLIST

Time: 5 minutes
Ease/difficulty: Easy
Hair type: Long and naturally curly or permed

You will need:
✔ widely spaced tooth comb
✔ covered band
✔ ponytail styler
✔ mousse

TIP
When inserting the styler through a ponytail, carefully move it from side to side in order to create enough room to pull the looped end of the styler through more easily.

FRENCH BRAID

This elegant, sophisticated braid looks complex, but it does get easier with practice.

1 Take a section of hair from the front of the head and divide into three strands.

2 Braid once; that is, take the right strand over the centre strand, the left over the centre, and the right over the centre.

3 Maintaining your hold on the braid with your fingers, use your thumbs to gather in additional hair (approximately 1 cm/½ in strips) from each side of the head and add these to the original strands. Braid the strands once again.

TIP
Shorter front layers can be woven into this type of braid, for example when growing out a fringe (bangs).

---

4 Continue in this way, picking up more hair as you continue down the braid. Secure with a covered band and add a scrunchie.

STYLING CHECKLIST

Time: 15–20 minutes
Ease/difficulty: Quite difficult
Hair type: Mid-length to long, and straight
You will need:
✔ covered band
✔ scrunchie

DOUBLE-STRANDED BRAIDS

These clever braids have a fishbone pattern, which gives an unusual look.

STYLING CHECKLIST

Time: 10 minutes
Ease/difficulty: Needs practice
Hair type: Long and straight

You will need:
✔ styling comb
✔ covered bands
✔ coloured feathers
✔ two short lengths of fine leather

1 Part your hair in the centre and comb it straight.

2 Divide the hair on one side of your head into two strands, then take a fine section from the back of the back strand and take it over to join the front strand, as shown.

3 Now take a fine section from the front of the front strand and cross it over to the back strand. Take a fine section from the back strand again and bring it over to join the front strand. Continue in this way; you will soon see the fishbone effect appear. Secure the ends with covered bands and add feathers, tying in place with fine leather. Repeat these three steps on the other side.

TOP KNOT

Ring the changes on finely braided locks by adding bright cord and tying the hair in a top knot.

1 Bind the end of each braid with cord, tying in a knot to secure.

2 Cross the braids over one another. Pick up and hold the braids from the crown section in either hand, as shown.

3 Tie in a knot.

4 Repeat step 3 so you have a double knot. Secure the knot with a decorative hairpin.

STYLING CHECKLIST

Time: 15–20 minutes
Ease/difficulty: Easy
Hair type: Long, finely braided or braided hair extensions

You will need:
✔ length of colourful cord about 5 m/5 yd long
✔ decorative hairpin

CROWN BRAIDS

By braiding the crown hair and allowing the remaining hair to frame the face you can achieve an interesting contrast of textures.

1 Clip up the top hair on one side of your head, leaving the back hair free. Take a small section of hair at ear level and comb it straight.

TIP
The volume of the curls can be increased by tipping your head forwards, then applying styling spray and scrunching the hair lying underneath.

2 Start braiding quite tightly, doing one cross (right strand over centre, left over centre), and gradually bring more hair into the outside strands.

3 Continue in this way, taking the braid towards the back of the head.

4 Make another parting about 2.5 cm/1 in parallel to and above the previous braid, and repeat the process. Continue in this way until all the front hair has been braided. Scrunch the remaining hair into loose curls to increase the volume. Finally, add a decorative Alice band.

STYLING CHECKLIST

Time: 15 minutes
Ease/difficulty: Needs practice
Hair type: Mid-length to long, and naturally curly or permed

You will need:
✔ large clip
✔ comb
✔ small covered bands
✔ Alice band

BASKET-WEAVE BRAID

You'll need to enlist the help of a friend to help you create this unusual braid.

1 Divide the hair into seven equal strands – three strands on either side of the face and one at the centre back.

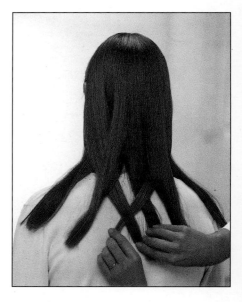

5 Take the third strand on the right-hand side over the central strand, and under the third strand on the left-hand side.

2 Starting at the right-hand side, cross the first strand (the strand nearest the face) over the second strand.

3 Cross the third strand over what is now the second strand, as shown.

4 Repeat steps 2 and 3 on the left side. What was originally the first strand in each group has now become the third strand.

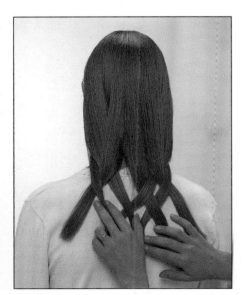

6 Now bring the first strand on the right-hand side over the second strand and under the central strand.

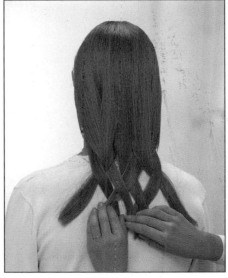

7 Repeat step 6 on the left side. Finally, clasp with a scrunchie.

DECORATED BRAIDS

Fine braids are quite time-consuming to do, but they can be left in place for many weeks.

1 Take small sections of hair, about 2.5 cm/1 in wide, and divide each section into three strands. Begin to braid.

STYLING CHECKLIST

Time: Depends on expertise, but even with practice it is time-consuming
Ease/difficulty: Quite easy
Hair type: Works well on Afro-Caribbean hair

You will need:
✔ tiny covered bands
✔ about 5 m/5 yd of fine gold ribbon

2 Continue braiding from the roots down to the ends.

3 Secure the ends with a covered band and decorate with fine gold ribbon. Repeat all round the head.

TIP
If you are leaving braids in for more than a few days, use a moisturizing spray to keep the scalp supple.

RICK-RACK BRAIDS

You can achieve a colourful style by braiding the hair with rick-rack to give a young, fresh style.

1 Braid the front of the hair as described for Crown Braids. Tie three strands of rick-rack together at one end and pin to the covered band of one braid.

2 Take a section of hair and divide it into three strands, aligning one piece of rick-rack with each strand.

3 Begin braiding, taking the right strand over the centre strand, the left over the centre, right over the centre, and so on.

4 Continue braiding down to the ends of the hair and tie the rick-rack to fasten.

TWIST AND COIL

This style starts with a simple ponytail, is easy to do, and looks stunning.

1 Smooth the hair back and secure in a ponytail using a covered band.

2 Divide off a small section of hair and mist with shine spray for added gloss.

3 Holding the ends of a section, twist the hair until it rolls back on itself to form a coil.

4 Position the coil in a loop as shown and secure in place using hairpins. Continue in this manner, until all the hair has been coiled. Decorate by intertwining with a strip of sequins.

STYLING CHECKLIST

Time: 10 minutes
Ease/difficulty: Easy
Hair type: Long, one length, straight hair

You will need:
✔ covered band
✔ shine spray
✔ hairpins
✔ 1 m/1 yd strip of sequins

CAMEO BRAID

A classic bun is given extra panache by encircling with a braid.

1 Smooth the hair into a ponytail and secure with a covered band, leaving one section of the hair free.

2 Place a bun ring over the ponytail.

3 Take approximately one-third of the hair from the ponytail and wrap it around the bun ring, securing with pins. Repeat with the other two-thirds of hair.

4 Braid the section of hair that was left out of the ponytail, right strand over centre strand, left over centre and so on, and wrap the braid around the base of the bun, then secure with pins.

STYLING CHECKLIST

Time: 10 minutes.
Ease/difficulty: Needs practice
Hair type: Long and straight

You will need:
✔ covered band
✔ bun ring
✔ hairpins

ROPE BRAID

A simple braid is entwined with rope to give an unusual finish.

1 Divide off the top section of hair and comb it through. Hold in place with a clip and pin the rope in place on the crown.

2 Separate the front piece of hair into three equal strands. Begin to braid.

3 When the braid reaches the top of the rope, merge a strand of rope with each strand of braid and continue working down to the ends.

4 Secure with a covered band. Make four more small braids, equally spaced around the head, and secure the ends with small covered bands.

STYLING CHECKLIST

Time: 10 minutes.
Ease/difficulty: Easy
Hair type: Long and straight

You will need:
✔ comb
✔ clip
✔ length of rope cut into equal pieces and tied at one end
✔ hairpin
✔ small covered bands

CITY SLICKER

Transform your hair in minutes using gel to slick it into shape and add sheen.

1 Take a generous amount of gel and apply it to the hair from the roots to the ends.

2 Use a vent brush, a comb or your fingers to distribute the gel evenly through the hair.

3 Comb the hair into shape using a styling comb to encourage movement.

TIP
Make sure you distribute the gel evenly all over your hair before styling.

4 Shape to form a quiff, and sleek down the sides and back.

STYLING CHECKLIST

Time: 5 minutes
Ease/difficulty: Easy
Hair type: Short crops

You will need:
✔ gel
✔ small vent brush
✔ styling comb

MINI BRAIDS

This young, fresh style is
perfect for teenagers.

2 Divide off a section at one side as shown and divide again into three equal parts.

1 Part the hair in the centre and smooth with a little wax that has first been warmed between the palms of your hands, before spreading over the hair.

3 Braid by placing the right strand over the centre strand, the left over the centre, right over the centre, and so on, pulling the braid slightly towards the face.

5 Part the back hair into four equal sections, from the crown down to the nape, and braid as shown. This time, start the braid at the top with three strands of hair and, after each turn of the braid, add in a small section of hair from each side. The easiest way to do this is to lift up these additional sections of hair with your little fingers.

4 Continue down to the ends of the hair and secure with a small covered band. Repeat on the other side.

6 Secure the ends of the braids with small covered bands and decorate the braids with ribbon bows.

BAND BRAID

STYLING CHECKLIST

Time: 5 minutes
Ease/difficulty: Easy
Hair type: Long, one length

You will need:
✔ brush
✔ covered band
✔ wax
✔ grip (pin)

A plain ponytail can be transformed by simply covering the band with a tiny braid.

1 Brush the hair back into a smooth, low ponytail, leaving a small section free for braiding. Secure in place with a covered band. Smooth the reserved section with a little styling wax.

2 Divide this section into three equal strands. Now, braid the hair in the normal way.

3 Take the braid and wrap it around the covered band ...

4 ...as many times as it goes. Finally, secure with a grip (pin).

CLIP UP

Long, curly hair can sometimes be unruly. Here's an easy way to tame tresses but still keep the beauty of the length.

1 Rub a little wax between the palms of your hands, then work into the curls with the fingertips. This helps give the curl separation and shine.

2 Take two interlocking large curved combs and use them to push the crown hair up towards the centre.

3 Push the teeth of the combs together to fasten.

TIP
It's much easier to disentangle curly hair if you use a comb with widely spaced teeth.

4 Repeat with two more combs at ear level to secure the back hair.

STYLING CHECKLIST

Time: 2 minutes
Ease/difficulty: Easy
Hair type: Mid-length to long, curly or straight

You will need:
✔ wax
✔ two sets of interlocking curved combs

DRAPED CHIGNON

This elegant style is perfect for that special evening out.

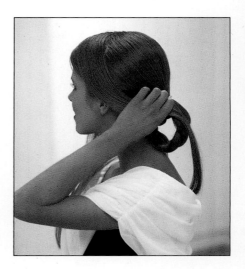

1 Part the hair in the centre from the forehead to the middle of the crown. Comb the side hair and scoop the back hair into a low ponytail using a covered band.

2 Loosely braid the ponytail – take the right strand over the centre strand, the left over the centre, the right over the centre, and so on, continuing to the end. Secure the end with a small band, then tuck the end under and around in a loop and secure.

3 Pick up the hair on the left side and comb it in a curve back to the ponytail loop.

4 Swirl this hair over and under the loop and secure with grips (pins). Repeat steps 3 and 4 on the right side.

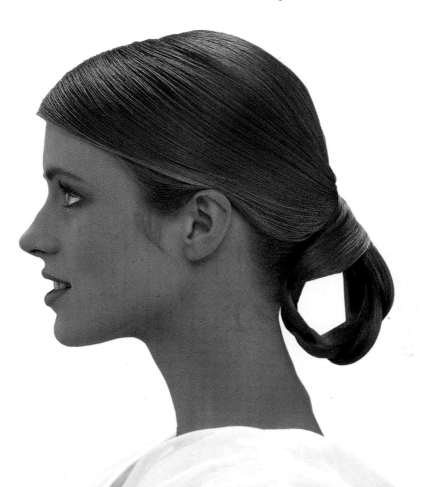

STYLING CHECKLIST

Time: 5–10 minutes
Ease/difficulty: Quite easy
Hair type: Long and straight

You will need:
✔ comb
✔ covered bands
✔ grips (pins)

TIP
Even long hair should be trimmed regularly, at least every two months.

UPSWEPT BRAIDS

Finely braided hair can be dressed up and decorated with sequins for a glamorous evening style.

1 Lift up the braids at the crown of the head and twist them around in one direction.

2 Secure in place with pins.

3 Gather up the remaining braids and loop them up to the crown.

TIP
Spray gloss misted over the braids will give a shine to the hair.

4 Pin in place and decorate by intertwining with sequins.

STYLING CHECKLIST

Time: 5–10 minutes
Ease/difficulty: Quite easy
Hair type: Long hair finely braided, or hair extensions

You will need:
✔ hairpins
✔ strip of fine sequins about 2 m/2 yd in all

SIMPLE PLEAT (ROLL)

Curly hair that is neatly pleated (rolled) gives a sophisticated style. The front is left full to soften the effect.

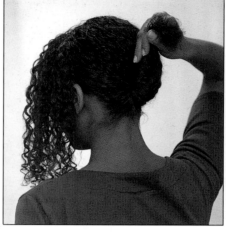

1 Divide off a section of hair at the front and leave it free. Smooth with a little serum. Take the remaining hair into one hand, as if you were going to make a ponytail.

2 Twist the handful of hair tightly from left to right.

3 When the twist is taut, turn the hair upwards as shown, to form a pleat (roll). Use your other hand to help smooth the pleat and at the same time neaten the top by tucking in the ends.

4 Secure the pleat (roll) with hair scroos or pins. Take the reserved front section, bring it back and secure it at the top of the pleat, allowing the ends to fall free.

STYLING CHECKLIST

Time: 5 minutes
Ease/difficulty: Quite easy
Hair type: Shoulder length or longer, curly or straight

You will need:
✔ serum
✔ hair scroos or pins

LOOPED CURLS

Two ponytails form the basis of this elegant style.

1 Apply setting lotion to the ends of the hair only. This will give just the right amount of body and bounce to help form the curls. Set the hair on heated rollers. When the rollers are quite cool – about 10 minutes after completing the set – take them out and allow the hair to fall free.

2 Divide off the crown hair and secure it with a covered band in a high ponytail. Apply a few drops of serum to add gloss, and brush the hair through.

3 Place the remaining hair in a lower ponytail.

4 Divide each ponytail into sections about 2.5 cm/1 in wide, then comb and smooth each section into a looped curl and pin in place. Set with hairspray.

STYLING CHECKLIST

Time: 10–15 minutes
Ease/difficulty: Needs practice
Hair type: Mid-length to long

You will need:
✔ setting lotion
✔ heated rollers
✔ covered bands, hairpins
✔ hairspray

FRENCH PLEAT (ROLL)

Mid-length to long hair can be transformed into a classic, elegant French pleat (roll) in a matter of minutes.

1 Backcomb the hair all over.

2 Smooth your hair across to the centre back and form the centre of the pleat (roll) by criss-crossing hair grips (pins) in a row from the crown downwards, as shown.

3 Gently smooth the hair around from the other side, leaving the front section free, and tuck the ends under.

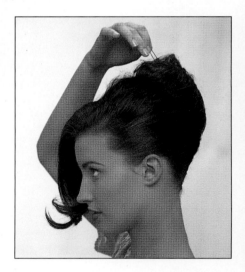

4 Secure with pins, then lightly comb the front section up and around to merge with the top of the pleat (roll). Mist with hairspray to hold.

STYLING CHECKLIST

Time: 5–10 minutes
Ease/difficulty: Quite easy
Hair type: Mid-length to long

You will need:
✔ comb
✔ hair grips (pins)
✔ hairpins
✔ hairspray

SHORT AND SPIKY

Short hair can be quickly styled using gel and wax to create a cheeky, fun look.

1 Work a generous amount of gel through your hair from the roots to the ends.

2 Dry your hair using a directional nozzle on your dryer; as you dry, lift sections of the hair to create height at the roots.

3 When the hair is dry, backcomb the crown to give additional height.

> **TIP**
> Gel can be re-activated by misting the hair with water and shaping it into style again.

4 To finish, rub a little wax between the palms of your hands, then apply it to the hair to give definition.

STYLING CHECKLIST

Time: 10 minutes
Ease/difficulty: Easy
Hair type: Short, layered and straight

You will need:
✔ gel
✔ dryer
✔ comb
✔ wax

FANTAIL

Add a streak of colour to a pretty ponytail twist.

1 Smooth your hair straight back using mousse to give sleekness. Hold the hair in one hand.

2 Take the clip-in hairpiece and push the small comb that is attached to the top, into the clasped hair.

3 Secure all your hair, including the hairpiece, in a covered band.

4 Twist and pin into place, fanning out the ends of your hair.

STYLING CHECKLIST

Time: 5 minutes
Ease/difficulty: Easy
Hair type: Long and straight

You will need:
✔ mousse
✔ clip-in coloured hairpiece
✔ covered band
✔ grips (pins)

UPSWEPT AND TOUSLED

A little backcombing and a simple twist creates this glamorous style.

1 The hair is diffuser-dried with the head held forward to give volume.

2 Take a section of hair and mist with styling spray.

3 Backcomb hair at the roots using a tail comb.

4 Repeat until all the crown hair is backcombed, then gather the length of hair to the back of the head and twist into a pleat (roll) and pin in place.

STYLING CHECKLIST

Time: 5 minutes
Ease/difficulty: Easy
Hair type: Mid-length, lightly layered

You will need:
✔ dryer with diffuser attachment
✔ styling spray
✔ tail comb
✔ grips (pins)

MINI HAIRPIECES

Give your hair instant colour
with mini clip-in hairpieces.

1 It is easier to put your hair up in
this style if it has been washed at
least one day before, as the hair's natural
grease makes it easier to handle.

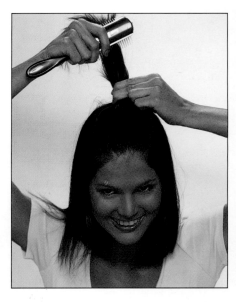

2 Use a styling brush to section off
the crown hair and secure as a small
ponytail using a covered band.

4 Brush the remaining hair in a third
section and secure with a covered
band in the same way.

5 Use a grip (pin) to attach a fine,
mini clip–in hairpiece to first
section of hair.

6 Twist hair round and pin in place
with a hairpin (barrette) to secure.

3 Take a second section of hair running from ear to ear and secure in a covered band in the same way.

7 Repeat with the second and third ponytails, using different coloured hairpieces. Leave the ends to splay out.

PIGTAIL CRIMP

Great for parties and discos, crimping adds extra interest to an upswept style.

1 The hair is shampooed, conditioned and left to dry naturally.

2 The fringe (bangs) is separated off and the hair centre-parted from forehead to nape. Brush one side of your hair upwards and secure in a ponytail.

3 Repeat for the other side.

4 Both ponytails are secured with covered bands.

5 Form one ponytail into a loop and thread the ends through a covered band, pulling them out for about 7.5 cm/ 3 in. Repeat with the other ponytail.

6 Secure looped hair with grips (barrettes).

8 Mist with hairspray.

TIP
Most crimping irons come with a
selection of plates – try using
different ones to create a mixture of
textures for an even more interesting
effect.

7 Starting with one section, hold the
hot crimping iron on one of the
loose sections of your hair. Keep the
tension for a few seconds and then
release the crimping plates. Move along
the section of hair and apply the
crimper again. Make sure that you line
up the crimping plates carefully to
ensure a uniform effect. Repeat, picking
sections of hair at random, including the
fringe (bangs) area.

MINI TWISTS

Pretty twists are decorated with slides (barrettes) for this fresh, young look.

1 The hair is blow-dried smooth with the ends flicked out.

2 Take a small section of hair and twist at the root, then mist with hairspray.

3 Secure with a hair slide (barrette).

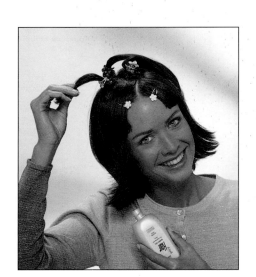

4 Repeat all over the head then make the ends sleek using smoothing gel.

STYLING CHECKLIST

Time: 5 minutes
Ease/difficulty: Easy
Hair type: Short/mid-length, fine to medium textured

You will need:
✔ hairspray
✔ selection of hair slides (barrettes)
✔ smoothing gel

TWIST AND CLIP

Short hair gets a fun new look by twisting and clipping sections up.

STYLING CHECKLIST

Time: 5 minutes
Ease/difficulty: Easy
Hair type: Short, fine and straight

You will need:
✔ selection of mini clips
✔ styling cream

1 Take small sections of hair and twist from the roots to the ends.

2 As you twist, the hair will double back on itself.

3 Secure hair with a mini clip.

4 When you have twisted and clipped all the crown hair, work a little styling cream into the ends to give a smooth finish.

QUICK TWISTS

Transform Afro hair quickly with this easy technique.

> **STYLING CHECKLIST**
>
> *Time:* 5–10 minutes
> *Ease/difficulty:* Easy
> *Hair type:* Afro or very curly
>
> *You will need:*
> ✔ mini clips
> ✔ serum
> ✔ liquid gel

1 Taking small sections of hair from the hairline to the crown, twist for three or four turns.

2 Secure with a mini clip, making sure you get the teeth of the clip on either side of the twist.

3 After you have completed a few sections, smooth on a little serum.

4 Hold the hair in place with a fine mist of liquid gel.

HEIDI BRAIDS

Simple three-strand braids are great teamed with flower slides (barrettes) and a fine hair-band.

1 From a centre parting, brush your hair smooth to the head.

2 Secure in two ponytails, one behind each ear.

3 Divide one ponytail into three equal strands and hold them apart.

4 Braid by taking the right strand over the centre strand, the left strand over the centre, and the right over the centre again, keeping the braid even.

5 Repeat to the end of your hair and secure the ends in a round slide (barrette). Do the same for other side and add a fine hair-band.

STYLING CHECKLIST

Time: 5 minutes
Ease/difficulty: Easy
Hair type: Straight, shoulder length

You will need:
✔ vent brush
✔ covered bands
✔ round slides (barrettes)
✔ fine hairband

SIMPLE PLEAT (ROLL)

It is really easy to put long hair up with the help of a pretty hair accessory.

1 Wash, shampoo and blow-dry your hair straight. Work a few drops of serum through the hair to make it easier to manage. The smoother your hair is to start with, the easier it will be to handle.

2 Use a styling brush to sleek your hair down to the nape of your neck.

3 Hold the hair in one hand and twist until it doubles back up on itself.

4 Secure by pushing the teeth of the comb hair accessory in place, just catching the hair centrally, but securing at the side of the twist of hair. Fan out the ends.

5 Mist the ends with hairspray to hold the look.

INSTANT COLOUR

Totally change your look by
applying instant colour that
washes out with the
next shampoo.

1 Dispense a little colour on to the
comb and work into the ends of
side hair.

2 Smooth the fringe (bangs) down
neatly so that it is flat.

3 Apply colour to the tips of the
fringe (bangs).

STYLING CHECKLIST

Time: 2 minutes
Ease/difficulty: Very
easy
Hair type: Any

You will need:
✔ instant hair colour
✔ styling comb

QUICK LIFT

Add height and volume to your hair by using this simple technique.

1 Take sections of your hair and mist with hairspray, then backcomb at the roots using a styling comb.

2 Take a section at a time of backcombed hair and twist and pin in place, leaving the ends sticking up.

3 Smooth the fringe (bangs) and side hair with styling cream.

TEXTURIZING

Very fine, hard-to-manage hair can be given texture and movement using this unusual technique.

STYLING CHECKLIST

Time: 10 minutes
Ease/difficulty: Quite easy
Hair type: Fine and straight

You will need:
✔ section clip
✔ styling spray
✔ flat irons

1 The hair is shampooed, conditioned and left to dry naturally.

2 Part your hair in the centre, clip the top hair out of the way and mist one section with styling spray.

3 Divide this section into three equal strands. Braid by taking the right strand over the centre strand, the left over the centre, and the right over the centre again, keeping the braid even. Repeat to the ends of your hair.

4 Mist the braid with styling spray.

5 Clasp the braid between flat irons to set the texture.

6 Repeat, working in the same manner all over the head.

7 Don't forget to do the back of your hair.

8 Leave your hair to cool completely, then unravel the braids one at a time and ruffle your hair with your fingers.

PERM REVIVAL

A perm that is growing out and has lost some bounce can be given a new lease of life using this step-by-step technique.

1 As a perm begins to grow out it loses lift and volume and can look flat.

2 Apply mousse, making sure it coats every strand of hair from the roots to the tips.

3 Gently dry the hair using the diffuser attachment on the dryer.

4 As the hair begins to dry, tilt your head forward to give maximum volume and root lift.

QUICK ALTERNATIVE

The back of the hair is twisted into a pleat (roll) at the centre and held with a clip. Photos: courtesy of Best Magazine.

FRIZZ CONTROL

Here's how to tame long, naturally curly hair that tends to go into a wild frizz.

1 The hair is shampooed, conditioned and left to dry naturally.

STYLING CHECKLIST

Time: 15 minutes
Ease/difficulty: Easy
Hair type: Naturally curly, mid-length to long

You will need:
✔ conditioner
✔ dryer with diffuser and nozzle attachments
✔ bristle brush
✔ styling spray
✔ heated rollers

2 Working on one small section of hair at a time, work conditioner into the hair so that it coats every strand from root to tip. Do not overload, but use enough to cover the outer layers of hair and make it feel silky.

SMOOTH ALTERNATIVE

3 Dry the conditioned curls with a diffuser attachment on the dryer, using a low heat and speed setting. Tip your head so that the hair falls into the diffuser cup and the gentle heat dries the hair. Do not ruffle the hair with your hands whilst drying.

1 Instead of leaving the hair to dry naturally, blow-dry with a bristle brush until it is smooth.

2 Mist the hair with styling spray and wind the front sections of hair on to heated rollers. Leave to cool completely, remove the rollers and brush hair into soft, curvy waves at the front. Photos: courtesy of Best Magazine.

CURL AND LIFT

Crimping the roots of curly hair gives a much fuller, wilder style.

1 The hair is shampooed and conditioned.

2 Work mousse all through the hair from the ends up to the roots making sure all the hair is covered.

4 The hair is diffuser-dried ready for crimping.

5 Working on one section of hair at a time, crimp the root area. Clasp the hair between the plates of the hot crimper and hold for a few seconds before releasing.

3 Dry the hair using the diffuser attachment on the dryer set at low heat and speed. Allowing the curls to sit in the diffuser cup encourages curl formation while the warm air gently dries the hair.

7 Continue in this manner, crimping the front area of your hair.

6 The first section of hair is crimped at the root.

8 Mist hair with styling spray and arrange with your fingers.

CURLY OPTIONS

Natural curls or permed hair can be styled in many different ways.

1 Curly hair that needs a lift can be given a quick transformation the day after shampooing.

2 Spray with curl reviver which helps to re-form movement.

3 Taking one section at a time, backcomb the roots, then tilt your head forward and mist with hairspray.

STYLING CHECKLIST

Time: 5 minutes
Ease/difficulty: Easy
Hair type: Naturally curly or permed, mid-length to long

You will need:
✔ curl reviver spray
✔ styling comb
✔ hairspray
✔ 2 foam bun rings
✔ clip

QUICK ALTERNATIVE

1 Open out one bun ring and pin it in place at the side of your head, then wrap a section of hair loosely around and pin it at the centre back. Repeat on the other side.

2 Loosely clip the front hair back, wrapping it round your fingers to get height. Leave tendrils at the sides and nape for a soft effect. Photos: courtesy of Best Magazine.

SPRINGY CURLS

Afro hair needs gentle drying to get the curls to frame the face.

1 The hair is shampooed, conditioned and left to dry naturally.

2 Work mousse through the hair from the roots to the ends.

3 Diffuser-dry the hair using a low heat and speed setting.

4 To arrange hair to frame your face, use a comb to flatten the hair round the hairline, whilst diffuser-drying.

STYLING CHECKLIST

Time: 5 minutes
Ease/difficulty: Easy
Hair type: Very curly, mid-length

You will need:
✔ mousse
✔ dryer with diffuser attachment
✔ styling comb

QUICK TRANSFORMATIONS

TRANSFORMATION 1

If you need a new look in a hurry, try these quick changes.

> ## STYLING CHECKLIST
>
> *Time:* 2 minutes
> *Ease/difficulty:* Easy
> *Hair type:* Short and straight
>
> *You will need:*
> ✔ small clip-in hairpiece in contrasting hair colour
> ✔ styling comb

Start with your hair blow-dried smooth and sleek. Separate the hair on the crown and attach a clip-in hairpiece, then comb your natural hair over.

TRANSFORMATION 2

> ## STYLING CHECKLIST
>
> *Time:* 1 minute
> *Ease/difficulty:* Very easy
> *Hair type:* Short, straight and layered
>
> *You will need:*
> ✔ instant colour gel
> ✔ styling comb

Style your hair, then dispense a little colour gel on to a comb and use to highlight areas of hair.

RINGING THE CHANGES

Don't get stuck in a rut with your hair – change the way you style it to get an instant new look.

1 The hair is shampooed, conditioned and roughly blow-dried.

2 Apply mousse and blow-dry, flicking the ends out.

3 Work wax through the hair and ruffle with your fingers.

4 Pin the top hair back and slick the sides behind your ears. Make a zigzag parting and smooth hair back with gel, clasping it at the back in a low ponytail. Photos: courtesy of Best Magazine.

STYLING CHECKLIST

Time: 5 minutes
Ease/difficulty: Easy
Hair type: Straight, layered cut

You will need:
✔ mousse
✔ dryer
✔ styling brush
✔ wax
✔ grips (barrettes)
✔ comb
✔ gel
✔ covered band

WAVE CONTROL

Natural waves can be feathered forward following this step-by-step technique.

1 Naturally wavy hair can sometimes be difficult to shape.

2 Shampoo and condition, then rough-dry using a round bristle brush to smooth out natural waves.

3 When the hair is almost dry, apply the styling spray.

4 Wind hair on to self-holding rollers, mist again with styling spray and leave for 10 minutes until completely dry. You can use a little heat at this point to speed things up if you wish. Remove the rollers and brush hair forward on to your face. Photos: courtesy of Best Magazine.

STYLING CHECKLIST

Time: 10 minutes
Ease/difficulty: Quite easy
Hair type: Naturally wavy with layered sides

You will need:
✔ round bristle brush
✔ dryer
✔ styling spray
✔ self-holding rollers

CURL AND CLIP

Transform curls by sweeping them up into this fun style.

1 Scoop one side of your hair up to the crown and hold it in place with one hand.

2 Secure with a decorative pin.

3 Repeat on the other side.

4 Mist the crown hair with styling spray and arrange the curls.

STYLING CHECKLIST

Time: 2 minutes
Ease/difficulty: Easy
Hair type: Very curly, mid-length

You will need:
✔ decorative pins
✔ styling spray

MINI FLICK-UPS

Turning out ends gives a fun look for short hair.

1 Shampoo, condition and rough-dry the hair, then apply styling spray.

2 Clip top layer of hair back. Use a round brush attachment on the air styler to build body into the sides of your hair.

3 Use a roller ball attachment on the air styler to give volume on the crown. Work down towards the ends, flicking the ends out as you move through the hair.

STYLING CHECKLIST

Time: 10 minutes
Ease/difficulty: Quite easy
Hair type: Mid-length, straight

You will need:
✔ styling spray
✔ section clip
✔ air styler
✔ serum

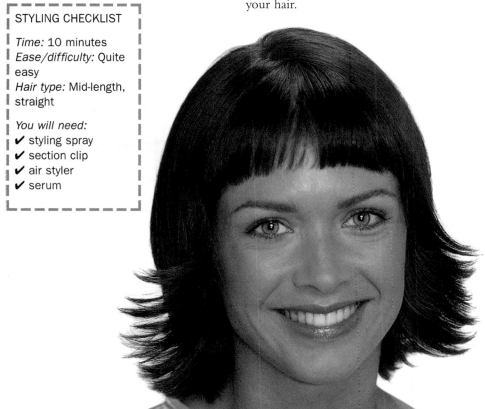

4 Work serum into the ends of the hair to give texture.

SLEEK AND GELLED

STYLING CHECKLIST

Time: 10 minutes
Ease/difficulty: Easy
Hair type: Fine and short

You will need:
✔ volumizing spray
✔ dryer with nozzle attachment
✔ styling brush
✔ small flat irons
✔ gel
✔ vent brush

Short hair can be quickly changed if you follow the step-by-step guide.

1 Short hair can easily be given body and sleekness.

2 Apply volumizing spray to the roots.

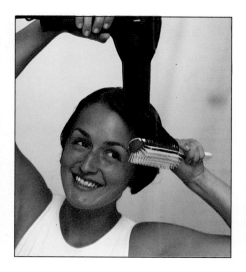

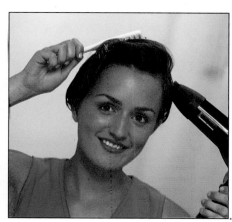

QUICK ALTERNATIVE

Gel is applied to the root area. Using a nozzle attachment on the dryer and a vent brush, the hair is smoothed into a quiff (flip) that curls on to the forehead.

3 Blow-dry the hair, a section at a time, using a styling brush.

4 Use small flat irons to run down sections of the hair. This will tame fly-away ends. Finally, brush the hair forwards. Photos: courtesy of Best Magazine.

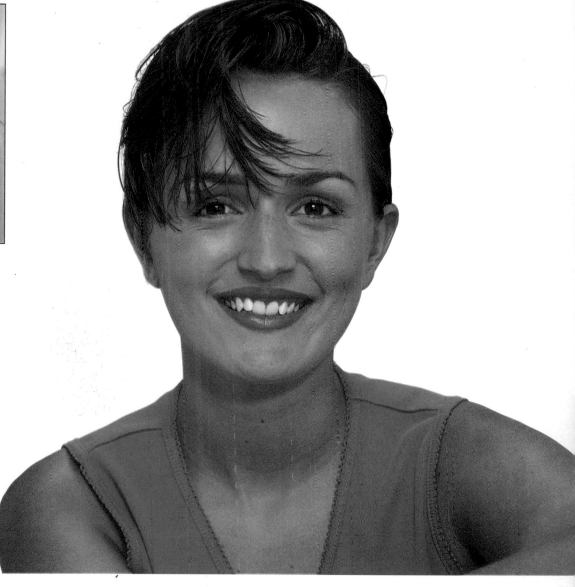

FULL OR SLICK

STYLING CHECKLIST

Time: 15 minutes
Ease/difficulty: Easy
Hair type: Naturally curly or permed, mid-length

You will need:
✔ curl revitalizer
✔ dryer with diffuser and nozzle attachments
✔ paddle brush

Permed or natural curls can be styled full, or smoothed into a classic bob.

1 Revitalize permed or naturally curly hair.

3 Dry hair using the diffuser attachment on the dryer. Allow hair to sit in the diffuser cup and do not ruffle or handle the hair too much or you will cause it to frizz. Photos: courtesy of Best Magazine.

QUICK ALTERNATIVE

Instead of diffuser-drying, smooth the hair in large sections using a paddle brush.

2 Shampoo and condition the hair, then spray with curl revitalizer, making sure to treat the root area which is where volume begins.

4 Smooth the front hair by lifting with your fingers and aiming the heat from the dryer with the nozzle attached.

WAVY OR SMOOTH

STYLING CHECKLIST

Time: 5–10 minutes
Ease/difficulty: Easy
Hair type: Fine and
wavy

You will need:
✔ curl revitalizer
✔ dryer with nozzle
attachment
✔ styling cream
✔ styling brush

Fine hair can be encouraged to
wave or be styled straight.

1 Natural waves can easily be shaped
into a new style.

3 Scrunch-dry your hair, using your
free hand to scrunch up handfuls of
hair at a time, until dry.

QUICK ALTERNATIVE

Instead of scrunching, blow-dry your hair using a styling brush and nozzle attachment on the dryer, aiming the heat downwards to get maximum shine.

2 Shampoo and condition the hair, then apply curl revitalizer all through the hair.

4 When your hair is dry, work some styling cream through the ends to give texture and separation. Photos: courtesy of Best Magazine.

TEXTURE AND VOLUME

Blow dry hair full or clip up for a stunning style

1 Shampoo and condition hair then comb through.

2 Use a vent brush to apply mousse from roots to ends.

STYLING CHECKLIST

Time: 10 minutes
Ease/difficulty: Easy
Hair type: Thick and straight

You will need:
✔ vent brush
✔ mousse
✔ dryer with concentrator nozzle
✔ paddle brush
✔ styling brush
✔ grips (pins)
✔ wax
✔ hairspray

QUICK ALTERNATIVE

For an elegant alternative take sections and twist then pin them in place on the crown. When complete mist with hairspray to hold the style.

3 Dry using a concentrator on dryer and a paddle brush to lift hair at the roots.

4 Switch to a styling brush and lift hair to create volume. Work a little wax through the outer layers of hair to give texture. Photos: courtesy of Denman.

SWEPT UP OR SMOOTH

Straight hair can be versatile if you follow the step-by-step guide to achieve two different looks.

1 Simple plaits can be transformed into more sophisticated styles.

2 Hair is shampooed, conditioned and rough-dried, using styling spray to give plenty of volume.

STYLING CHECKLIST

Time: 10 minutes
Ease/difficulty: Easy
Hair type: Straight, slightly layered

You will need:
✔ styling spray
✔ dryer
✔ hair grips (barrettes)
✔ paddle brush

3 Movement is created by rolling the hair in your hand and aiming heat on that area.

4 See how much texture is achieved with this simple process. Hair is then pinned up at random. Photos: courtesy of Best Magazine.

QUICK ALTERNATIVE

Instead of rough-drying, smooth the hair with a paddle brush after shampooing and conditioning.

STRAIGHT AND FEATHERED

Medium textured hair can be blow-dried straight or set on rollers for instant movement.

STYLING CHECKLIST

Time: 15 minutes
Ease/difficulty: Quite easy
Hair type: straight or slightly wavy

You will need:
✔ mousse
✔ paddle brush
✔ dryer
✔ round bristle brush
✔ styling spray
✔ self-holding rollers

1 The hair is shampooed and conditioned, then combed through.

2 Apply mousse to the hair using a paddle brush to distribute the mousse evenly from the roots to ends.

4 Switch to a round thermo bristle brush and continue smoothing the hair straight and smooth. Photos: courtesy of Denman

3 Begin to blow-dry your hair, using the paddle brush to lift it at the roots.

QUICK ALTERNATIVE

Mist your hair with styling spray then divide into sections and wind onto self–holding thermo rollers. Heat the set hair for 10 minutes. Remove the rollers and lightly brush through.

THE WEDDING

Short bobs look stunning worn
smooth and sleek and dressed
with a simple tiara.

1 Shampoo, condition and partially
dry the hair to remove most of the
moisture.

2 Using a barrel brush attachment on
an air styler, smooth the hair down
section by section to give a sleek finish.
Add a pretty tiara and adjust your make-up.

STYLING CHECKLIST

Time: 15 minutes
Ease/difficulty: Easy
Hair type: Short, one-length bob

You will need:
✔ dryer
✔ air styler
✔ tiara

For a softer style, the hair is gently curled into romantic curls.

1 Scrunch-dry your hair to create movement and volume.

2 Next, curl the hair section by section, using a large barrel brush attachment on an air styler. This will smooth the curls and give an even fuller look. As each section is completed, pin it into a curl and leave to set until you have finished all the remaining hair. Remove the pins and brush through gently – curls and movement will spring into shape. Pin fresh flowers into the hair to add the finishing touch.

Hair Denise McAdam, London, using Philips Haircare Appliances. Make-up Jenny Jordan. Photography Iain Philpott.

STYLING CHECKLIST

Time: 10–15 minutes
Ease/difficulty: Quite easy
Hair type: Short, one length bob

You will need:
✔ dryer with diffuser attachment
✔ air styler with large barrel brush attachment
✔ hairpins
✔ brush
✔ fresh flowers

COUNT DOWN TO THE BIG DAY

❍ Two or three weeks beforehand get your hair into condition with a series of intensive conditioning treatments.

❍ Once you have chosen your dress, experiment with different hairstyles. You might like to take photographs so you can compare the results before deciding which is the right style for you.

❍ Perms, highlights or all-over colour should be done about two weeks before the wedding. If you choose a longer-lasting semi-permanent, this can be done a week before.

Long hair is swept up into sophisticated curls.

1 Shampoo and condition your hair. Dry the hair using a medium heat setting on the dryer. The medium setting is gentle and caring for longer hair.

2 Put your hair up into a high ponytail and curl into loops, as described in step 4 in Looped Curls. Pin in place. Curl short lengths of hair using an air styler fitted with a tong attachment. Just lift the depressor, wrap the hair around the barrel, hold for a few seconds, and then release the curl. Pin the tiara in place and attach the veil to the back of the head.

Hair Denise McAdam, London, using Philips Haircare Appliances. Make-up Jenny Jordan. Photography Iain Philpott.

STYLING CHECKLIST

Time: 10–15 minutes
Ease/difficulty: Needs practice
Hair type: Long and straight or naturally wavy

You will need:
✔ dryer
✔ covered band
✔ pins
✔ air styler with tong attachment
✔ tiara
✔ veil

For a very feminine look, the hair is delicately curled to fall in a mass of waves.

1 Shampoo, condition, and dry the hair. Fit the tong attachment on to the air styler and wrap the hair around the barrel, taking care not to buckle the ends of the hair. Hold for a few minutes, then release the curl. Pin it up and work on the next piece of hair. Continue in this way until you have tonged the whole head.

2 Release the curls and allow them to fall free. Recurl any strands that need it, then to give added separation and freedom to the curls, use a hairdryer with a diffuser attachment. Set the dryer on a low heat/speed setting and gently ruffle the hair. This will increase the volume as well as separating the curls. To finish, clip back the hair and secure with a flower band.

STYLING CHECKLIST

Time: 20 minutes
Ease/difficulty: Needs practice

You will need:
✔ air styler with tong attachment
✔ dryer with diffuser
✔ flower band

WIGS AND HAIRPIECES

Change your image in an instant with a wig or a hairpiece; it's a simple, quick, and effective way to change your looks.

The model, with her short urchin cut.

A classic *coupe sauvage* wig feathers on to the face.

All wigs and hairpieces by René of Paris, The Designer Wig Collection, Trendco, London.

Above: A wig styled in a short bob gives a neat head shape. *Left:* For instant length and glamour try a long, blonde wig.

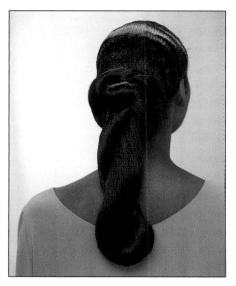

When adding hairpieces, first slick the hair back into a tight ponytail, either high on the crown or at the nape, depending on the look you want to achieve.

Above: Two long hairpieces are used for this style. The first is attached to a low ponytail, twisted, and then pinned up. The second is coiled around to form a bun.

Above: Pre-curled hairpieces are clipped to a high ponytail, with some hair wound around and secured with two scrunchies.

Two curly hairpieces are pinned to a high ponytail.

Braided hairpieces are coiled around to form a high chignon.

CUSTOMIZING A WIG

Wigs can be purchased at department stores, but for the best result ask your hairdresser to customize the style to suit your face shape and features.

1 Natural hair is smoothed back and the wig pulled into place.

2 The top hair is clipped up and the side hair is razor cut to feather forward.

5 After the first section is completed, the hair is then razored round the nape of the neck.

4 A further section is brought down and razor cut, following the line.

3 The edges are cut straight using scissors.

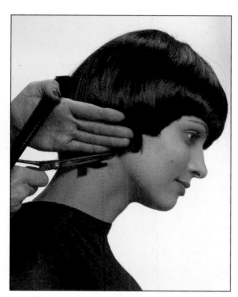

6 The other side is cut in the same way.

7 The edges are neatened with scissors.

CLIP-IN HAIRPIECES

Clip-in coloured hairpieces can be used to dramatically change your look in minutes.

1 Add brightness to long, straight hair. First shampoo, condition and towel-dry the hair.

2 Use a round, metal-barrelled styling brush to smooth the hair a section at a time.

3 Get your hair really straight by running the steam straightening irons down each section of hair.

4 Mist with hairspray to control any stray ends.

5 Colour hairpieces, or wefts, have tiny fixing combs so they can be attached to the hair.

6 Part your hair in the centre, then make another parting parallel with the first one, as shown. Hold this section of hair up.

7 Align a hairpiece with the second parting and push the clip into place before combing the natural hair over. Repeat on the other side. Photos: courtesy of Best Magazine.

For a quick change, twist the back hair into a pleat (roll) and clip it with a large clip. Comb the side hair straight and leave to fall free.

FALSE FRINGES (BANGS)

Clip-in false fringes (bangs) provide an easy way to change your hair without cutting.

1 Take a section of hair at the crown as shown and hold it in one hand.

2 Clip the fringe (bangs) along the parting using the pins that are fitted on to the edge of the hairpiece.

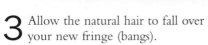

3 Allow the natural hair to fall over your new fringe (bangs).

4 Smooth the hair using flat irons.

ACCESSORIES

Nothing becomes a hairstyle quite like hair accessories. Bandeaux, ribbons and bows come into their own at party time, but they can also be used at any time to transform your hair – instantly.

SCRUNCHIES

Scrunchies are elasticated bands that are covered with a tube of fabric, which ruches up when it is placed over a ponytail. They are available in a variety of fabrics including fine, pleated silks and soft chiffons.

Left: A scrunchie completely alters the appearance of Twist and Coil.

BEADS

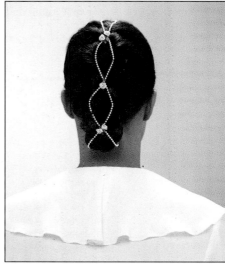

Above: The French Braid is tucked up and decorated with a strip of tiny pearls and small fabric flowers.

Beads can be threaded on to strands of hair for special looks, and many accessories are, in fact, made of hundreds of small beads.

BENDIES

Above: A bendy used as a headband.

Bendies are long pieces of flexible wire encased in fabric - often velvet or silk - that can be twisted into the hair in a variety of eye-catching ways; for example, as a band, braided into a ponytail, entwined round a bun, or bound on to a braid. They come in many different colours and materials.

BOWS

Above: A floppy bow adds instant sparkle to our Draped Chignon.

Bows can be tailored or floppy, and are usually made from soft silks and velvets attached to a slide (barrette).

FLOWERS

Above: Fresh flowers are pinned into the style Twist and Braid.

For special occasions, especially weddings, fresh flowers are perfect. However, if you want to keep your flowers afterwards, use some of the beautiful silk alternatives.

HEADBANDS

Above: Add a beaded headband and a scrunchie to hair fastened in a low bun.

Headbands come in a wide variety of fabrics and widths. Classic colours such as black, navy, red, cream and tortoiseshell are good basics.

SLIDES, CHIGNON PINS, COMBS

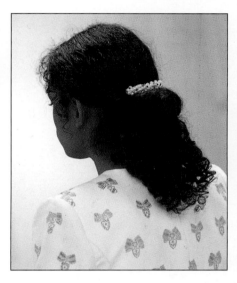

Above: A pearl slide (barrette) gives added interest to Curly Styler.

Unusual slides and barrettes are excellent for finishing off a braid or adding interest to a ponytail. Chignon pins add instant sophistication and are a means of securing buns. Combs can be used to lift the hair off the face, allowing the hair to fall free, but not in your eyes.

Curly hair is versatile too, if you
choose the right accessory.

Pin the hair back with
jewelled slide clips.

Add elegance with a pearl–
threaded covered band.

Pin artificial flowers on top
of an upswept style.

For a very feminine touch
add a pretty bow slide ...

... or an embroidered and
bejewelled ribbon.

For the evening, clip a classic
bow among the curls ...

...or let the feathers fly.

Left: Intertwine a gold and
a black bendy and use as a
headband.

Accessories Head Gardener,
London.

Many of the styles created in the Successful Styling and Hair Dressing sections can be transformed in seconds by adding a pretty hair accessory.

Long straight hair can be dressed with a wide range of accessories to suit every occasion.

A classic snood with bow is used to gather up Decorated Braids.

The Cameo Braid is transformed by the addition of a snood.

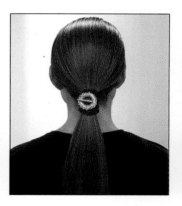

Try a pretty clip ...

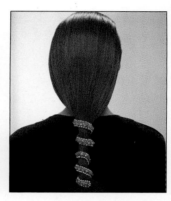

... or a simple beaded twist.

A black chiffon bow and a diamanté pin add another dimension to the Draped Chignon.

Simple but stunning: three chiffon scarves are braided and wound round a ponytail.

Make a ponytail, twist it and flip it up, then secure with a glittery band and three decorated clips.

This extravagant hair-band could double as a hat.

Left: Braids can be clipped up on to the crown and the ends clasped in a scrunchie.

Position flower bands down a length of ponytail ...

... or use curved clips decorated with ribbons and a matching scrunchie.

Accessories Head Gardener, London.

Covered bendies enable you to create a variety of styles.

Gather the top part of the hair into a ponytail and fit the bendy around in a twist. Make one cross with the bendy, then incorporate the lower hair into a braid. Squeeze the end of the bendy to secure.

For this style, simply fold the end of the hair and bendy under and press again.

Effect another transformation by bending the end up and securing it at the crown.

Put hair into a ponytail, then place one end of the bendy over to finish.

Accessories Head Gardener, London.

Left: Fit the band around the head, cross the ends over to gather the hair into a ponytail, then bend the ends to finish as shown.

Slides (Barrettes)

Choose diamanté (rhinestones) to complement waves.

Brightly coloured clips for a feathered effect.

A simple butterfly clip contrasts with blonde hair.

Secure hair at the nape with a mass of slides (barrettes).

Spider slides (barrettes) can be scattered over upswept hair ...

... used to enhance a sleeker look ...

... or formed into a pretty row.

Clips, combs and bands

To clip up tonged curls ... front ...

... and back view.

A comb instantly sweeps up curls.

A band holds curls back from the face.

Tiaras

Twisted metal and diamanté (rhinestone).

A pop-art metallic crown tiara.

Simple waves of diamanté (rhinestone) snake through the hair.

A small tiara completes an upswept style.

Fake flowers

Form a focal point on upswept looks.

Use a single bloom ...

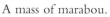

... or maybe two.

Accessories: Head Gardener, London.

Feathers and fake fur and hair

A simple braid of fake fur.

Balls of fur blend beautifully with contrasting hair colours.

A mass of marabou.

Ebony feathers.

Feathers are fixed to long hair pins.

INDEX